READ UP on Content Areas 3

NE_Build & Grow

Unit Components

Building Background Knowledge

prepares students for the reading passage by providing additional topic information and visual aids.

On Your Own

applies points from the text to students' lives.

The Big Question

prompts students to think about the main idea of the passage.

Visual Aids

provide more information about the main text and help students understand the passage with additional illustrations and photographs.

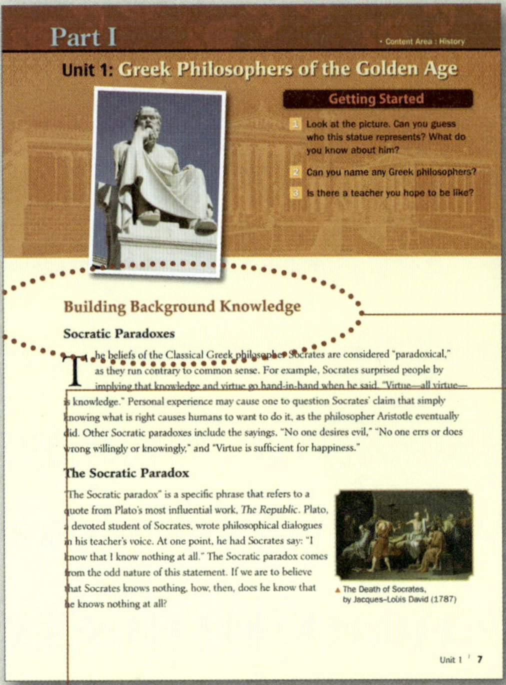

Part I · Content Area : History

Unit 1: Greek Philosophers of the Golden Age

Getting Started

1. Look at the picture. Can you guess who this statue represents? What do you know about him?
2. Can you name any Greek philosophers?
3. Is there a teacher you hope to be like?

Building Background Knowledge

Socratic Paradoxes

The beliefs of the Classical Greek philosopher Socrates are considered "paradoxical," as they run contrary to common sense. For example, Socrates surprised people by implying that knowledge and virtue go hand-in-hand when he said, "Virtue—all virtue—is knowledge." Personal experience may cause one to question Socrates' claim that simply knowing what is right causes humans to want to do it, as the philosopher Aristotle eventually did. Other Socratic paradoxes include the sayings, "No one desires evil," "No one errs or does wrong willingly or knowingly," and "Virtue is sufficient for happiness."

The Socratic Paradox

"The Socratic paradox" is a specific phrase that refers to a quote from Plato's most influential work, *The Republic*. Plato, a devoted student of Socrates, wrote philosophical dialogues in his teacher's voice. At one point, he had Socrates say: "I know that I know nothing at all." The Socratic paradox comes from the odd nature of this statement. If we are to believe that Socrates knows nothing, how, then, does he know that he knows nothing at all?

▲ The Death of Socrates, by Jacques-Louis David (1787)

Unit 1 | 7

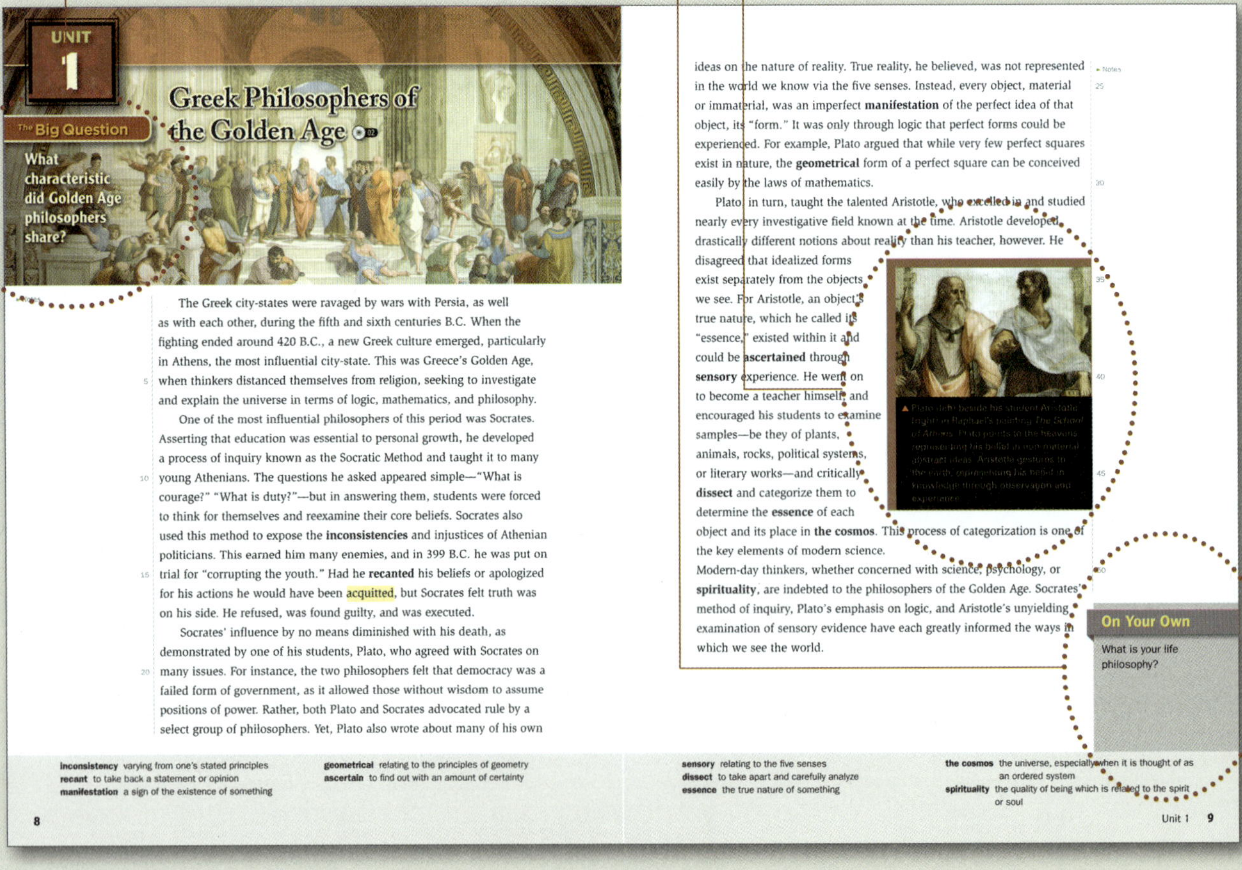

UNIT 1

Greek Philosophers of the Golden Age

The Big Question

What characteristic did Golden Age philosophers share?

The Greek city-states were ravaged by wars with Persia, as well as with each other, during the fifth and sixth centuries B.C. When the fighting ended around 420 B.C., a new Greek culture emerged, particularly in Athens, the most influential city-state. This was Greece's Golden Age, when thinkers distanced themselves from religion, seeking to investigate and explain the universe in terms of logic, mathematics, and philosophy.

One of the most influential philosophers of this period was Socrates. Asserting that education was essential to personal growth, he developed a process of inquiry known as the Socratic Method and taught it to many young Athenians. The questions he asked appeared simple—"What is courage?" "What is duty?"—but in answering them, students were forced to think for themselves and reexamine their core beliefs. Socrates also used this method to expose the **inconsistencies** and injustices of Athenian politicians. This earned him many enemies, and in 399 B.C. he was put on trial for "corrupting the youth." Had he **recanted** his beliefs or apologized for his actions he would have been acquitted, but Socrates felt truth was on his side. He refused, was found guilty, and was executed.

Socrates' influence by no means diminished with his death, as demonstrated by one of his students, Plato, who agreed with Socrates on many issues. For instance, the two philosophers felt that democracy was a failed form of government, as it allowed those without wisdom to assume positions of power. Rather, both Plato and Socrates advocated rule by a select group of philosophers. Yet, Plato also wrote about many of his own ideas on the nature of reality. True reality, he believed, was not represented in the world we know via the five senses. Instead, every object, material or immaterial, was an imperfect **manifestation** of the perfect idea of that object, its "form." It was only through logic that perfect forms could be experienced. For example, Plato argued that while very few perfect squares exist in nature, the **geometrical** form of a perfect square can be conceived easily by the laws of mathematics.

Plato, in turn, taught the talented Aristotle, who excelled in and studied nearly every investigative field known at the time. Aristotle developed drastically different notions about reality than his teacher, however. He disagreed that idealized forms exist separately from the objects we see. For Aristotle, an object's true nature, which he called its "essence," existed within it and could be **ascertained** through **sensory** experience. He went on to become a teacher himself, and encouraged his students to examine samples—be they of plants, animals, rocks, political systems, or literary works—and critically **dissect** and categorize them to determine the **essence** of each object and its place in **the cosmos**. This process of categorization is one of the key elements of modern science.

Modern-day thinkers, whether concerned with science, psychology, or **spirituality**, are indebted to the philosophers of the Golden Age. Socrates' method of inquiry, Plato's emphasis on logic, and Aristotle's unyielding examination of sensory evidence have each greatly informed the ways in which we see the world.

▲ Plato (left) beside his student Aristotle (right) in Raphael's painting *The School of Athens*. Plato points to the heavens, representing his belief in non-material abstract ideas. Aristotle gestures to the earth, confirming his belief in knowledge through observation and experience.

Notes

On Your Own

What is your life philosophy?

inconsistency varying from one's stated principles
recant to take back a statement or opinion
manifestation a sign of the existence of something
geometrical relating to the principles of geometry
ascertain to find out with an amount of certainty
sensory relating to the five senses
dissect to take apart and carefully analyze
essence the true nature of something
the cosmos the universe, especially when it is thought of as an ordered system
spirituality the quality of being which is related to the spirit or soul

8 · Unit 1 9

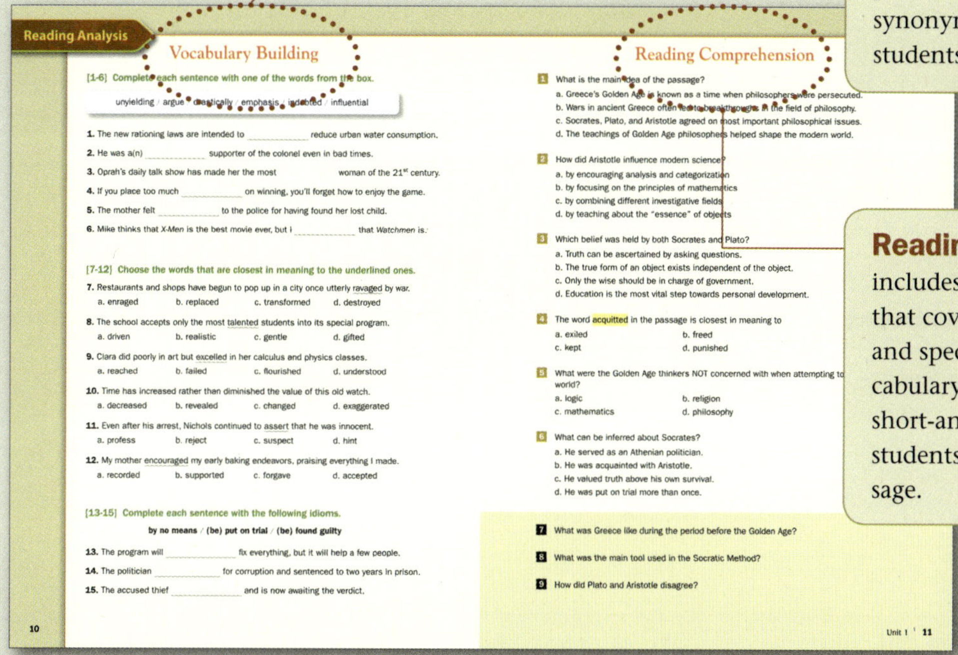

Reading Analysis

Vocabulary Building

[1-6] Complete each sentence with one of the words from the box.

unyielding / argue / drastically / emphasis / indebted / influential

1. The new rationing laws are intended to ____________ reduce urban water consumption.
2. He was a(n) ____________ supporter of the colonel even in bad times.
3. Oprah's daily talk show has made her the most ____________ woman of the 21st century.
4. If you place too much ____________ on winning, you'll forget how to enjoy the game.
5. The mother felt ____________ to the police for having found her lost child.
6. Mike thinks that *X-Men* is the best movie ever, but I ____________ that *Watchmen* is.

[7-12] Choose the words that are closest in meaning to the underlined ones.

7. Restaurants and shops have begun to pop up in a city once utterly ravaged by war.
   a. enraged b. replaced c. transformed d. destroyed
8. The school accepts only the most talented students into its special program.
   a. driven b. realistic c. gentle d. gifted
9. Clara did poorly in art but excelled in her calculus and physics classes.
   a. reached b. failed c. flourished d. understood
10. Time has increased rather than diminished the value of this old watch.
   a. decreased b. revealed c. changed d. exaggerated
11. Even after his arrest, Nichols continued to assert that he was innocent.
   a. profess b. reject c. suspect d. hint
12. My mother encouraged my early baking endeavors, praising everything I made.
   a. recorded b. supported c. forgave d. accepted

[13-15] Complete each sentence with the following idioms.

by no means / (be) put on trial / (be) found guilty

13. The program will ____________ fix everything, but it will help a few people.
14. The politician ____________ for corruption and sentenced to two years in prison.
15. The accused thief ____________ and is now awaiting the verdict.

10

Reading Comprehension

1 What is the main idea of the passage?
a. Greece's Golden Age is known as a time when philosophers were persecuted.
b. Wars in ancient Greece often led to breakthroughs in the field of philosophy.
c. Socrates, Plato, and Aristotle agreed on most important philosophical issues.
d. The teachings of Golden Age philosophers helped shape the modern world.

2 How did Aristotle influence modern science?
a. by encouraging analysis and categorization
b. by focusing on the principles of mathematics
c. by combining different investigative fields
d. by teaching about the "essence" of objects

3 Which belief was held by both Socrates and Plato?
a. Truth can be ascertained by asking questions.
b. The true form of an object exists independent of the object.
c. Only the wise should be in charge of government.
d. Education is the most vital step towards personal development.

4 The word acquitted in the passage is closest in meaning to
a. exiled b. freed
c. kept d. punished

5 What were the Golden Age thinkers NOT concerned with when attempting to world?
a. logic b. religion
c. mathematics d. philosophy

6 What can be inferred about Socrates?
a. He served as an Athenian politician.
b. He was acquainted with Aristotle.
c. He valued truth above his own survival.
d. He was put on trial more than once.

7 What was Greece like during the period before the Golden Age?

8 What was the main tool used in the Socratic Method?

9 How did Plato and Aristotle disagree?

Unit 1 11

Vocabulary Building

presents new words in context, synonyms, and idioms to improve students' vocabulary.

Reading Comprehension

includes multiple-choice questions that cover the main idea, general and specific information, and vocabulary. Negative, inference, and short-answer questions further test students' understanding of the passage.

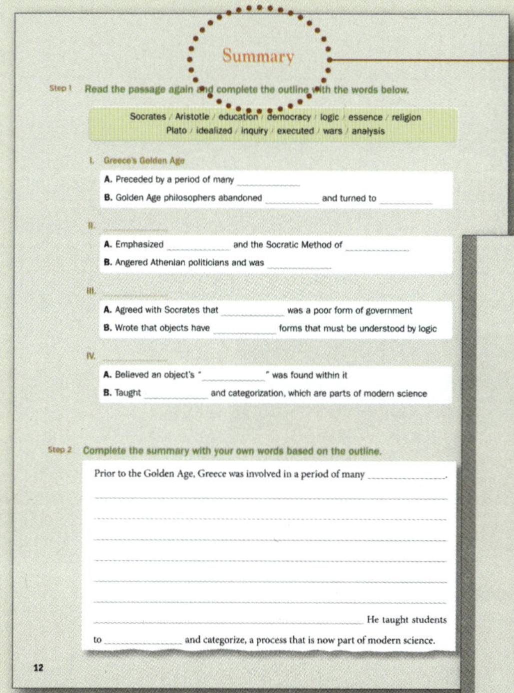

Summary

Step 1 Read the passage again and complete the outline with the words below.

Socrates / Aristotle / education / democracy / logic / essence / religion
Plato / idealized / inquiry / executed / wars / analysis

I. Greece's Golden Age
A. Preceded by a period of many ____________
B. Golden Age philosophers abandoned ____________ and turned to ____________

II. ____________
A. Emphasized ____________ and the Socratic Method of ____________
B. Angered Athenian politicians and was ____________

III. ____________
A. Agreed with Socrates that ____________ was a poor form of government
B. Wrote that objects have ____________ forms that must be understood by logic

IV. ____________
A. Believed an object's "____________" was found within it
B. Taught ____________ and categorization, which are parts of modern science

Step 2 Complete the summary with your own words based on the outline.

Prior to the Golden Age, Greece was involved in a period of many ____________.

He taught students to ____________ and categorize, a process that is now part of modern science.

12

Summary

Step 1 Completing an outline

Step 2 Writing a summary based on the information from Step 1

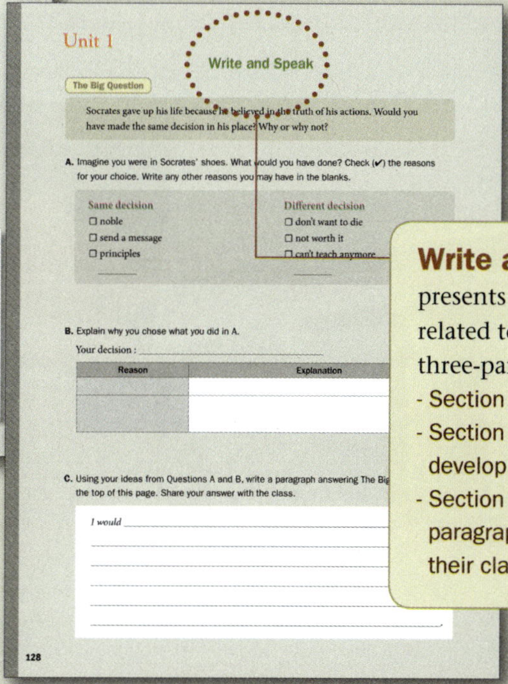

Unit 1

Write and Speak

The Big Question

Socrates gave up his life because he believed in the truth of his actions. Would you have made the same decision in his place? Why or why not?

A. Imagine you were in Socrates' shoes. What would you have done? Check (✔) the reasons for your choice. Write any other reasons you may have in the blanks.

Same decision	Different decision
☐ noble	☐ don't want to die
☐ send a message	☐ not worth it
☐ principles	☐ can't teach anymore

B. Explain why you chose what you did in A.

Your decision : ____________

Reason	Explanation

C. Using your ideas from Questions A and B, write a paragraph answering The Big the top of this page. Share your answer with the class.

I would ____________

128

Write and Speak

presents students with a question related to the passage followed by a three-part writing exercise.

- Section A is a warm-up activity
- Section B helps students form and develop their ideas
- Section C asks students to write a paragraph that they will share with their class

Contents

Part I

UNIT	CONTENT AREA		TITLE	PAGE
1	Social Studies	History	Greek Philosophers of the Golden Age	7
2		History	The Age of Discovery	13
3	Science	Earth Science	Our Shifting Earth	19
4		Life Science	Dance Language Among Honey Bees	25
5	Cross Curricular	History & Science	The Invention of the Modern Printing Press	31

Part II

UNIT	CONTENT AREA		TITLE	PAGE
6	Social Studies	History	Decoding the Rosetta Stone	37
7		Economics	The Great Depression	43
8	Science	Earth Science	Understanding Hurricanes	49
9		Life Science	What Are GMOs?	55
10	Cross Curricular	Life Science & History	The History of Salt	61

Part III

UNIT	CONTENT AREA		TITLE	PAGE
11	Social Studies	History	The Cultural Advances of Hellenism	67
12		History	Impressionism	73
13	Science	Earth Science	The Great Barrier Reef	79
14		Earth Science	The Frozen Continent	85
15	Cross Curricular	History & Technology	The Birth of the Skyscraper	91

Part IV

UNIT	CONTENT AREA		TITLE	PAGE
16	Social Studies	Life Science	The Placebo Effect	97
17		Economics	Greenwashing	103
18	Science	Earth Science	Predicting Volcanic Eruptions	109
19		Earth Science	A Star is Born	115
20	Cross Curricular	Art, Science & History	Inventing the "Talkie"	121

Supplementary Material (Write & Speak) 127

Vocabulary List 148

Part I

• Content Area : History

Unit 1: Greek Philosophers of the Golden Age

Getting Started

1 Look at the picture. Can you guess who this statue represents? What do you know about him?

2 Can you name any Greek philosophers?

3 Is there a teacher you hope to be like?

Building Background Knowledge

Socratic Paradoxes

The beliefs of the Classical Greek philosopher Socrates are considered "paradoxical," as they run contrary to common sense. For example, Socrates surprised people by implying that knowledge and virtue go hand-in-hand when he said, "Virtue—all virtue—is knowledge." Personal experience may cause one to question Socrates' claim that simply knowing what is right causes humans to want to do it, as the philosopher Aristotle eventually did. Other Socratic paradoxes include the sayings, "No one desires evil," "No one errs or does wrong willingly or knowingly," and "Virtue is sufficient for happiness."

The Socratic Paradox

"The Socratic paradox" is a specific phrase that refers to a quote from Plato's most influential work, *The Republic*. Plato, a devoted student of Socrates, wrote philosophical dialogues in his teacher's voice. At one point, he had Socrates say: "I know that I know nothing at all." The Socratic paradox comes from the odd nature of this statement. If we are to believe that Socrates knows nothing, how, then, does he know that he knows nothing at all?

▲ The Death of Socrates, by Jacques–Louis David (1787)

UNIT 1

Greek Philosophers of the Golden Age

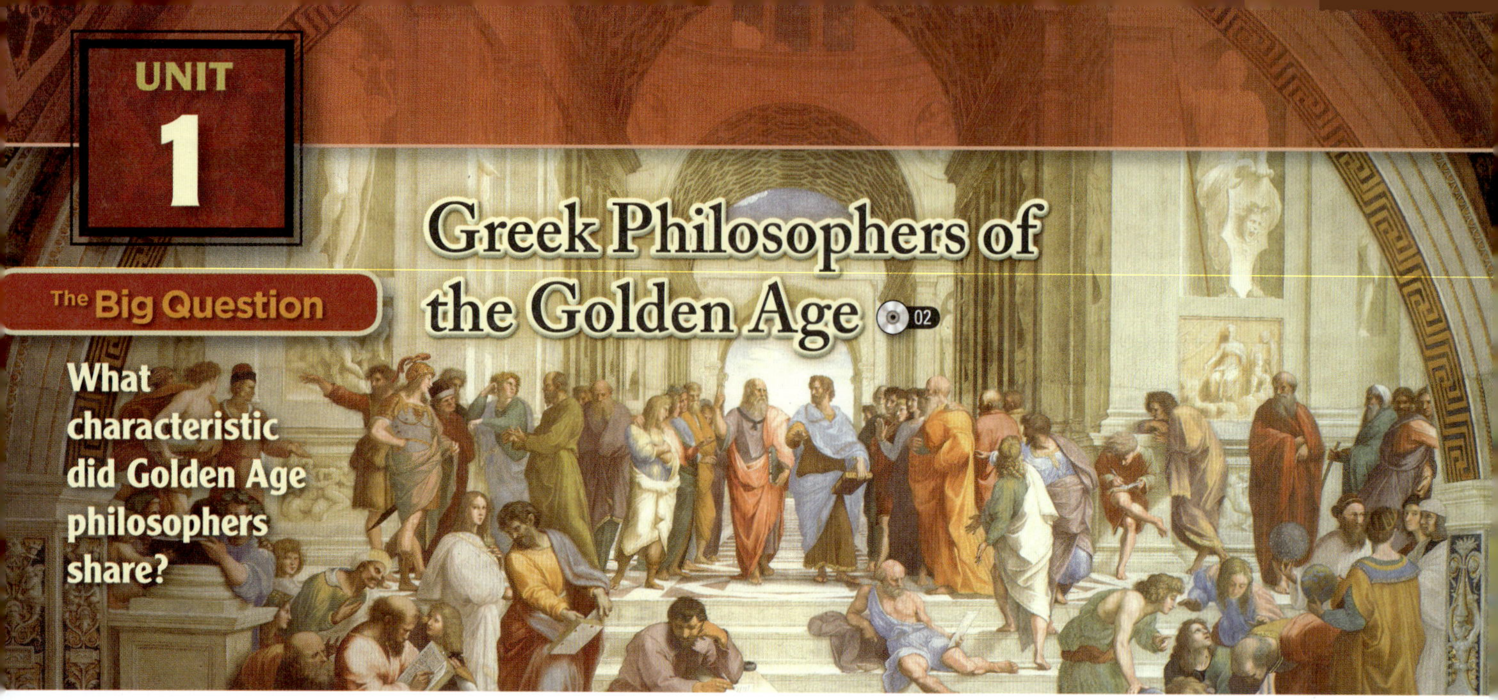

The Big Question

What characteristic did Golden Age philosophers share?

► Notes

The Greek city-states were ravaged by wars with Persia, as well as with each other, during the fifth and sixth centuries B.C. When the fighting ended around 420 B.C., a new Greek culture emerged, particularly in Athens, the most influential city-state. This was Greece's Golden Age, when thinkers distanced themselves from religion, seeking to investigate and explain the universe in terms of logic, mathematics, and philosophy.

One of the most influential philosophers of this period was Socrates. Asserting that education was essential to personal growth, he developed a process of inquiry known as the Socratic Method and taught it to many young Athenians. The questions he asked appeared simple—"What is courage?" "What is duty?"—but in answering them, students were forced to think for themselves and reexamine their core beliefs. Socrates also used this method to expose the **inconsistencies** and injustices of Athenian politicians. This earned him many enemies, and in 399 B.C. he was put on trial for "corrupting the youth." Had he **recanted** his beliefs or apologized for his actions he would have been acquitted, but Socrates felt truth was on his side. He refused, was found guilty, and was executed.

Socrates' influence by no means diminished with his death, as demonstrated by one of his students, Plato, who agreed with Socrates on many issues. For instance, the two philosophers felt that democracy was a failed form of government, as it allowed those without wisdom to assume positions of power. Rather, both Plato and Socrates advocated rule by a select group of philosophers. Yet, Plato also wrote about many of his own

inconsistency varying from one's stated principles
recant to take back a statement or opinion
manifestation a sign of the existence of something
geometrical relating to the principles of geometry
ascertain to find out with an amount of certainty

► Notes

ideas on the nature of reality. True reality, he believed, was not represented in the world we know via the five senses. Instead, every object, material or immaterial, was an imperfect **manifestation** of the perfect idea of that object, its "form." It was only through logic that perfect forms could be experienced. For example, Plato argued that while very few perfect squares exist in nature, the **geometrical** form of a perfect square can be conceived easily by the laws of mathematics.

Plato, in turn, taught the talented Aristotle, who excelled in and studied nearly every investigative field known at the time. Aristotle developed drastically different notions about reality than his teacher, however. He disagreed that idealized forms exist separately from the objects we see. For Aristotle, an object's true nature, which he called its "essence," existed within it and could be **ascertained** through **sensory** experience. He went on to become a teacher himself, and encouraged his students to examine samples—be they of plants, animals, rocks, political systems, or literary works—and critically **dissect** and categorize them to determine the **essence** of each object and its place in **the cosmos**. This process of categorization is one of the key elements of modern science.

▲ Plato (left) beside his student Aristotle (right) in Raphael's painting *The School of Athens*. Plato points to the heavens, representing his belief in non-material abstract ideas. Aristotle gestures to the earth, representing his belief in knowledge through observation and experience.

Modern-day thinkers, whether concerned with science, psychology, or **spirituality**, are indebted to the philosophers of the Golden Age. Socrates' method of inquiry, Plato's emphasis on logic, and Aristotle's unyielding examination of sensory evidence have each greatly informed the ways in which we see the world.

On Your Own

What is your life philosophy?

sensory relating to the five senses
dissect to take apart and carefully analyze
essence the true nature of something
the cosmos the universe, especially when it is thought of as an ordered system
spirituality the quality of being which is related to the spirit or soul

Vocabulary Building

[1-6] **Complete each sentence with one of the words from the box.**

unyielding / argue / drastically / emphasis / indebted / influential

1. The new rationing laws are intended to ____________ reduce urban water consumption.

2. He was a(n) ____________ supporter of the colonel even in bad times.

3. Oprah's daily talk show has made her the most ____________ woman of the 21st century.

4. If you place too much ____________ on winning, you'll forget how to enjoy the game.

5. The mother felt ____________ to the police for having found her lost child.

6. Mike thinks that *X-Men* is the best movie ever, but I ____________ that *Watchmen* is.

[7-12] **Choose the words that are closest in meaning to the underlined ones.**

7. Restaurants and shops have begun to pop up in a city once utterly <u>ravaged</u> by war.
a. enraged b. replaced c. transformed d. destroyed

8. The school accepts only the most <u>talented</u> students into its special program.
a. driven b. realistic c. gentle d. gifted

9. Clara did poorly in art but <u>excelled</u> in her calculus and physics classes.
a. reached b. failed c. flourished d. understood

10. Time has increased rather than <u>diminished</u> the value of this old watch.
a. decreased b. revealed c. changed d. exaggerated

11. Even after his arrest, Nichols continued to <u>assert</u> that he was innocent.
a. profess b. reject c. suspect d. hint

12. My mother <u>encouraged</u> my early baking endeavors, praising everything I made.
a. recorded b. supported c. forgave d. accepted

[13-15] **Complete each sentence with the following idioms.**

by no means / (be) put on trial / (be) found guilty

13. The program will ____________ fix everything, but it will help a few people.

14. The politician ____________ for corruption and sentenced to two years in prison.

15. The accused thief ____________ and is now awaiting the verdict.

Reading Comprehension

1 What is the main idea of the passage?

a. Greece's Golden Age is known as a time when philosophers were persecuted.
b. Wars in ancient Greece often led to breakthroughs in the field of philosophy.
c. Socrates, Plato, and Aristotle agreed on most important philosophical issues.
d. The teachings of Golden Age philosophers helped shape the modern world.

2 How did Aristotle influence modern science?

a. by encouraging analysis and categorization
b. by focusing on the principles of mathematics
c. by combining different investigative fields
d. by teaching about the "essence" of objects

3 Which belief was held by both Socrates and Plato?

a. Truth can be ascertained by asking questions.
b. The true form of an object exists independent of the object.
c. Only the wise should be in charge of government.
d. Education is the most vital step towards personal development.

4 The word acquitted in the passage is closest in meaning to

a. exiled b. freed
c. kept d. punished

5 What were the Golden Age thinkers NOT concerned with when attempting to understand the world?

a. logic b. religion
c. mathematics d. philosophy

6 What can be inferred about Socrates?

a. He served as an Athenian politician.
b. He was acquainted with Aristotle.
c. He valued truth above his own survival.
d. He was put on trial more than once.

7 What was Greece like during the period before the Golden Age?

8 What was the main tool used in the Socratic Method?

9 How did Plato and Aristotle disagree?

Summary

Step 1 **Read the passage again and complete the outline with the words below.**

Socrates / Aristotle / education / democracy / logic / essence / religion
Plato / idealized / inquiry / executed / wars / analysis

I. Greece's Golden Age

A. Preceded by a period of many ____________

B. Golden Age philosophers abandoned ____________ and turned to ____________

II. ____________

A. Emphasized ____________ and the Socratic Method of ____________

B. Angered Athenian politicians and was ____________

III. ____________

A. Agreed with Socrates that ____________ was a poor form of government

B. Wrote that objects have ____________ forms that must be understood by logic

IV. ____________

A. Believed an object's "____________" was found within it

B. Taught ____________ and categorization, which are parts of modern science

Step 2 **Complete the summary with your own words based on the outline.**

Prior to the Golden Age, Greece was involved in a period of many ____________.

____

____

____

____

____

____

____ He taught students to ____________ and categorize, a process that is now part of modern science.

Unit 2: The Age of Discovery

Getting Started

1. What are some good things and bad things about traveling by ship?
2. If you could travel somewhere, where would you go and why?
3. Do you know about any European explorers? What did they do?

Building Background Knowledge

Christopher Columbus

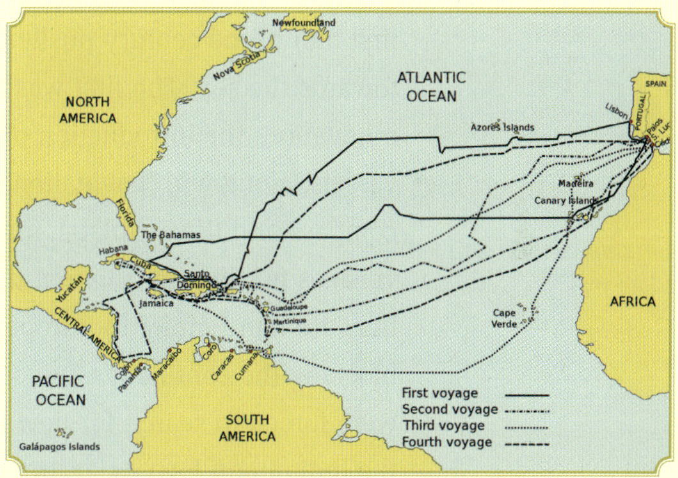

▲ Voyages of Christopher Columbus

Christopher Columbus was an explorer who was born in 1451 in Genoa, Italy. He believed that he could find a new way to reach the Indies by sailing west across the Atlantic Ocean. He proposed his plan for a new trade route to John II, the king of Portugal, who refused. Columbus made the same request to the king of Portugal several years later, but was rejected a second time. He was also turned down in Genoa and Venice, Italy.

Following nearly seven long years of negotiations, Spain's King Ferdinand and Queen Isabella accepted his proposal, hoping to use the new trade route to buy spices and silk from the East. On August 3, 1492, Columbus and his crew of 85 men set sail from Palos, Spain, in three ships named the *Nina*, the *Pinta*, and the *Santa Maria*.

After several rough weeks at sea, the exhausted crew spotted land, and on October 12, 1492, they stepped foot on an island in what is now the Bahamas, located in the Atlantic Ocean just north of Cuba.

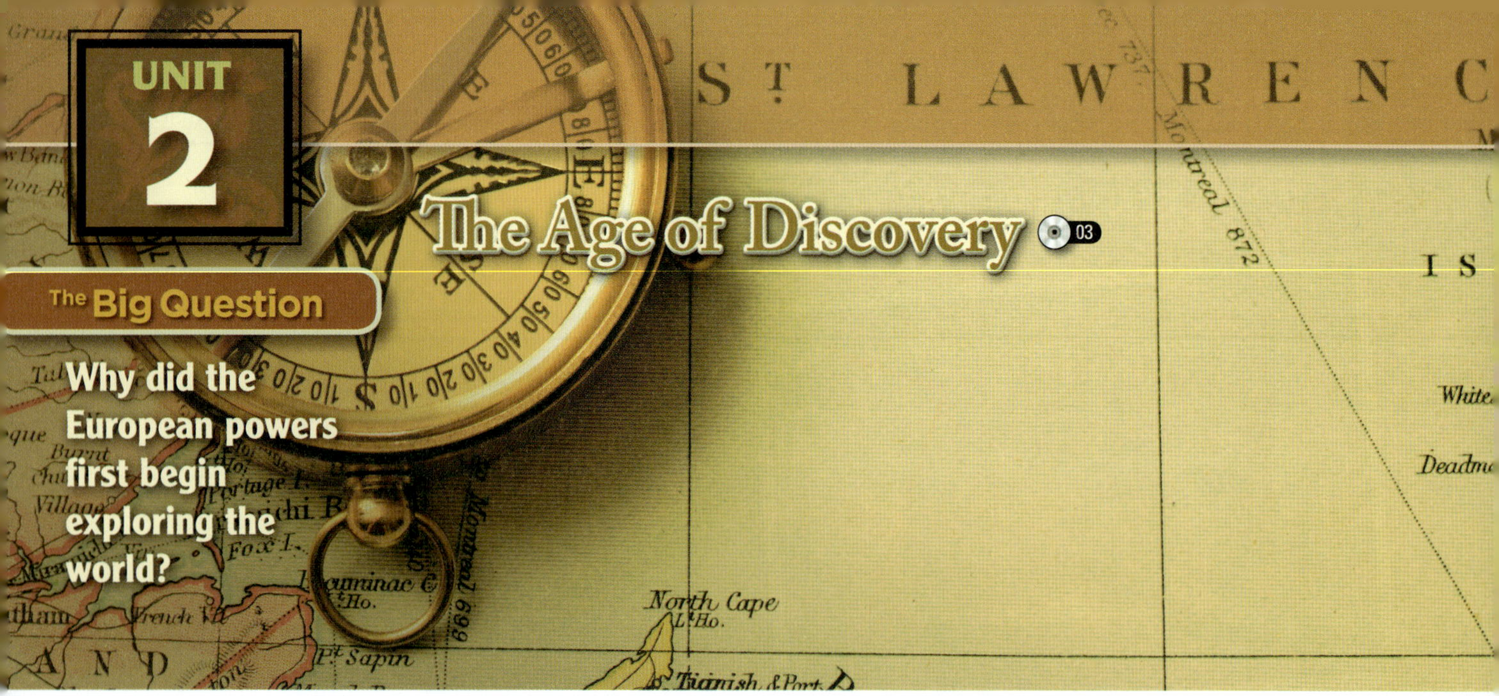

UNIT 2

The Age of Discovery

The Big Question

Why did the European powers first begin exploring the world?

► Notes

The year 1450 A.D. began a three-century era called "the Age of Discovery" that would see European influence spread throughout the globe. The **impetus** for this expansionism was commerce. European trade at the start of the 15th century was carried out primarily via land routes to India and the Far East, with gold, silver, silk, and spices being the products in highest demand. Two trends during the first half of the century pushed the Europeans towards the sea. The first was technological innovation; the introduction of improved sailing vessels, along with navigational tools like the compass and the astrolabe, made open-ocean voyages **feasible** for the first time. Secondly, the Ottoman Empire to Europe's southeast was blocking the continent's access to **overland trade**. By 1450, Europeans were forced to search for new maritime routes if they wanted to acquire the Indian and East Asian treasures they desired.

▲ Astrolabe

Portugal and Spain were the first to actively pursue this **endeavor**. While attempting to reach India by sailing across the Atlantic under Spanish sponsorship in 1492, the Italian explorer Christopher Columbus landed on an island in the Caribbean Sea. This was the discovery of the "New World," lands that would **feature prominently** in the story of European expansionism in the centuries to come. In 1497, the Portuguese explorer Vasco de Gama carried out the first successful voyage from

impetus a force that stimulates a process or activity
feasible capable of being done
overland trade commercial activity, especially between Europe and Asia
endeavor an attempt to do something in order to reach a goal
feature to be a distinctive part of

▸ Notes

Europe to India by sailing around the southern tip of Africa. And in 1522, an **expedition** led by Ferdinand Magellan, another Spanish-funded explorer, completed an around-the-world voyage, signifying Europe's global presence.

For several decades, Spain and Portugal remained the major players on the world scene. Spain managed to conquer the advanced native civilizations of present-day Mexico and South America, and both established trading posts throughout India, China, and Southeast Asia. At the same time, **explorations** were begun by three other European powers: Britain, France, and the Netherlands. Each **charted** vast areas of North America, hoping to find a northern sea passage to Asia. Though this prize did not exist, the three went on to claim portions of North America for their kings and reached Asia by other routes.

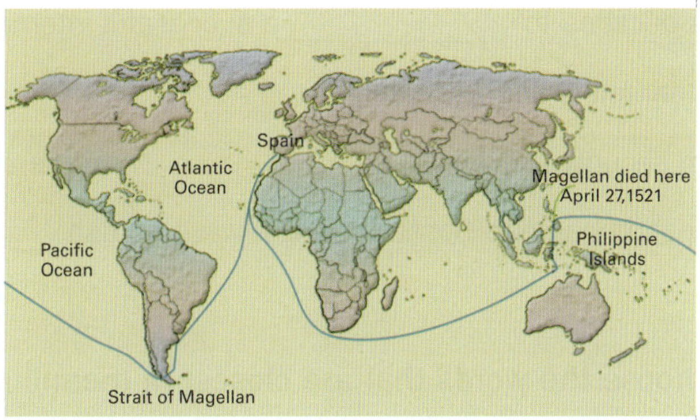

▲ Magellans's voyage around the world

In the 16th and 17th centuries, the wealth acquired from their newly conquered territories transformed the European kingdoms into overseas empires. The Americas proved rich sources of gold and silver, while Asian trade routes gave Europeans nearly unlimited access to the valuable spice trade. Colonies were founded all over the world to oversee the **extraction** and shipment of raw materials, and Europeans settled them in the tens of thousands, bringing their languages, religions, technologies, and cultural identities with them. Many effects of this mass migration were beneficial: a system of global trade was developed that eventually connected people and ideas from all over the world. Other consequences were not as positive: entire cultures were eradicated, especially in the New World, and the colonies' labor demands gave rise to an international slave trade. The Age of Discovery eventually led to the Age of Imperialism, when an empire came to be seen as a precursor to wealth and its size was thought to represent a nation's status.

On Your Own

Spices were once much more valuable than they are today. What is your favorite spice? Do you know how much it costs?

prominently in a major or important way
expedition a journey made for a specific purpose
exploration the process of visiting an unknown territory for the purpose of discovery
chart to methodically traverse
extraction the process of getting something, especially when some effort is involved

Vocabulary Building

[1-6] Complete each sentence with one of the words from the box.

establish / migration / transform / claim / beneficial / impact

1. The fast-increasing population will ____________ the small town into a huge city.

2. The U.S. housing crisis had a severe ____________ on the global economy.

3. It takes decades to ____________ a successful international hotel chain.

4. The winner fell ill and was unable to ____________ her prize at the awards ceremony.

5. Random security checks will be ____________ to the safety of all passengers.

6. My ancestors came to Boston during a wave of Irish ____________ in the 19th century.

[7-12] Choose the words that are closest in meaning to the underlined ones.

7. Real Madrid <u>acquired</u> Cristiano Ronaldo from Manchester United in 2009.

a. starred b. got into c. lured d. obtained

8. People from many different fields worked together to <u>pursue</u> a common goal.

a. commit b. release c. reserve d. seek

9. The dark colors used in this series of paintings <u>signify</u> the artist's somber mood.

a. invite b. imitate c. please d. indicate

10. Our organization was <u>founded</u> in 1999 for the purpose of aiding the poor.

a. moved b. purchased c. reviewed d. established

11. One <u>consequence</u> of the natural disaster was the loss of historical monuments.

a. opportunity b. result c. promise d. risk

12. No matter what we do, we are unable to <u>eradicate</u> this hardy colony of ants.

a. inquire b. contain c. destroy d. accept

[13-15] Complete each sentence with the following idioms.

give rise to / carry out / along with

13. She received a medal for having ____________ her duties with distinction.

14. Some disinfectants may ____________ dangerous antibiotic-resistant forms of bacteria.

15. When I go camping, I always bring a simple first-aid kit ____________ me.

Reading Comprehension

1 What is the main idea of the passage?

a. Each of Europe's powers undertook global exploration at the same time.

b. The effects of Europe's expansive policies were primarily negative.

c. Europeans' search for commerce caused their influence to spread worldwide.

d. The European kingdoms were obsessed with finding a maritime route to Asia.

2 What did the voyages of Columbus and those of Britain, France, and the Netherlands have in common?

a. They were trying to locate a westward route to Asia.

b. They were looking for gold and silver in the Americas.

c. They received financial support from Spain and Portugal.

d. They discovered new passageways to India and East Asia.

3 Which European power funded the first expedition to circle the world?

a. Portugal b. Spain

c. England d. France

4 The word oversee in the passage is closest in meaning to

a. benefit b. process

c. manage d. imply

5 Which of the following was NOT an initial reason for Europeans to explore the oceans?

a. an Ottoman Empire blockade

b. improvements in sailing technology

c. a chance to discover new lands

d. the promise of more direct trade routes

6 What can be inferred about sea voyages prior to the compass and the astrolabe?

a. Europeans chose not to undertake them.

b. Ships did not sail very far away from land.

c. Most were launched by the Ottoman Empire.

d. They had no commercial purpose.

7 How was the impact of Europe's expansionism both positive and negative?

8 Who were mainly responsible for exploring and claiming North American lands?

9 What was Vasco de Gama's contribution to the expansion of Europe?

Summary

Step 1 **Read the passage again and complete the outline with the words below.**

loss / trade / wealth / Columbus / advances / Portugal
Mexico / spread / North American / positively / expansion

I. Europe's ____________

A. Began in 1450, spurred by a desire for ____________

B. Resulted from technological ____________ and the ____________ of overland routes due to the Ottoman Empire

II. ____________ and Spain

A. Sent out the voyages of ____________, de Gama, and Magellan

B. Conquered lands in ____________ and South America and founded Asian colonies

III. Britain, France, and the Netherlands

A. Explored and claimed ____________ lands

B. Also reached Asia and engaged in trade

IV. The ____________ of European influence

A. ____________ from trade led to colonies and mass migration

B. Both ____________ and negatively, expansion helped shape the modern world

Step 2 **Complete the summary with your own words based on the outline.**

The period of Europe's expansion began in 1450, spurred by a desire for better ______ opportunities. ____

____

____

____

____

____

_____ Both ________ and negatively, this expansion helped shape the modern world.

Unit 3: Our Shifting Earth

Getting Started

1 Look at the picture. What do you see? What is Earth made of?

2 How can Mother Nature affect the Earth?

3 Can you think of a few ways in which human activities can change the Earth?

Building Background Knowledge

Pangaea

As recently as 250 million years ago, all of the continents were joined together in a super-continent called Pangaea. Pangaea broke up into continents which began drifting apart from one another 180 million years ago, a phenomenon which continues to occur today. Initially, Pangaea divided into Laurasia and Gondwana, which then broke up into North America, Europe, Asia, South America, Africa, Antarctica, and Australia. Looking at the current shapes of the continents, you can see how they may have once fit together.

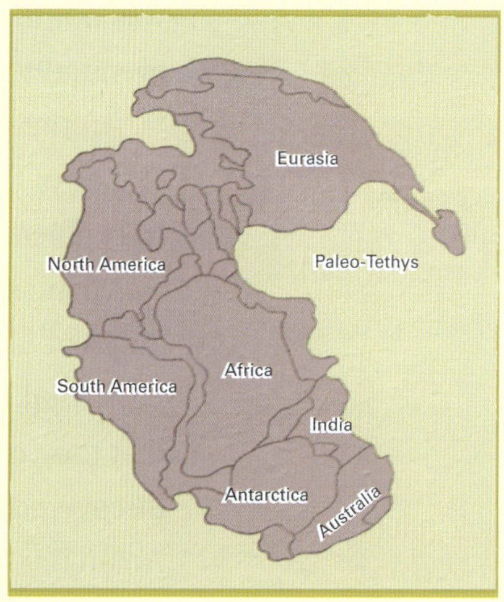

▲ Map of Pangaea

Presently, North America and South America are moving away from Europe and Africa, causing the Atlantic Ocean to grow in size and the Pacific Ocean to become smaller. Additionally, the Pacific Ocean is crashing against the western side of North America, which produces earthquakes in the state of California and forms the Rocky Mountains. Several hundred million years from now, the Pacific Ocean may disappear completely as the West Coast of North America smashes into Japan and China, creating another large continent and possibly a new mountain range.

UNIT 3

Our Shifting Earth

04

The Big Question

What does the theory of plate tectonics tell us about Earth?

► Notes

If you looked at a world map from 250 million years ago, you probably would not recognize it, for the positions of Earth's landmasses relative to one another in the distant past bore little resemblance to their **configuration** today. In other words, they are not **stationary**. As early as 1600 A.D., curious thinkers had suggested that the continents might be moving, remarking that certain coastlines, such as those of eastern South America and western Africa, appeared to fit together like puzzle pieces. It was not until the 20th century, however, that a theory was elaborated and eventually proven.

In the early 1900s, the German scientist Alfred Wegener **hypothesized** that all of the continents had once been connected but later drifted away from each other. He conducted research to determine whether this outlandish idea was plausible, collecting and comparing rock samples from the edges of different landmasses. He learned that rocks from eastern South America possessed the same geological **makeup** as those from western Africa, and that they contained fossils of the same prehistoric species as well. He also discovered fossils of tropical species buried in the **frigid** wasteland of Antarctica.

Wegener developed a theory of continental drift to explain his findings. In it, he formalized his idea that Earth's landmasses had been joined in a supercontinent, which he called Pangaea. Continents now separated by oceans had once existed side by side, accounting for their geological and biological similarities. Pangaea subsequently broke apart, and Earth's

configuration the relative positions of parts of a whole
stationary incapable of changing position
hypothesize to create a theory about something
make up physical qualities that combine to form a being
frigid very cold in temperature

continents gradually assumed their present configuration. Unfortunately, Wegener was unable to **theorize** what force could possibly be driving the movement of continents, and continental drift was dismissed by the scientific community.

During the 1950s and 1960s, three decades after Wegener's death, scientists started to reexamine continental drift due to advances in marine **sonar** technology. This equipment produced detailed maps of the ocean floor and the unexpected discovery of massive ridges under the sea. These submerged mountain chains were created by hot magma–liquid rock spouting up from beneath Earth's crust. As it cooled and hardened, the magma became new crust, and at a speed of about four inches per year, this crust traveled away from either side of the ridge.

Study of mid-ocean ridges led geologists to formulate the theory of plate tectonics. They hypothesized that Earth's crust was divided into multiple plates, each containing a portion of ocean, continent, or both and floating freely atop the liquid magma of Earth's interior. Where two oceanic plates moved away from one another, magma rose to the surface, forming new earth. Where two continental plates collided, they crumpled and pushed each other upwards to build the planet's great mountain ranges. Plate tectonics became the foundational principle in the field of **geology**, and it also confirmed Wegener's theory of continental drift, demonstrating the **mechanism** by which landmasses move. Geologists now believe Pangaea was simply the latest in a long progression of supercontinents that have formed and split, a process that will continue through future **eons**.

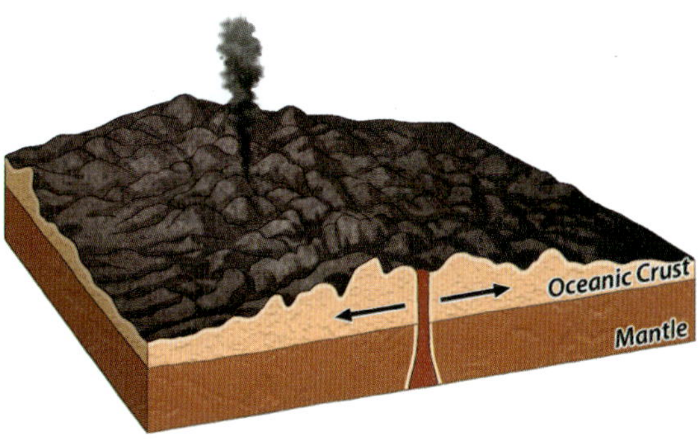

▸ Notes

On Your Own

What are some geographical features of your country? How do you think plate tectonics contributed to it?

theorize to form a theory about
sonar a technique used to locate objects underwater
geology the study of rocks and Earth's physical history
mechanism the method by which something occurs
eon an extremely long period of time

Vocabulary Building

[1-6] Complete each sentence with one of the words from the box.

ridge / spout / submerged / confirm / massive / prehistoric

1. The huge crater could only have been produced by a ______________ asteroid.

2. These hot springs regularly ______________ water and steam hundreds of feet into the air.

3. Ancient caves provide the only insight we have into the lives of ______________ humans.

4. Doctors are able to ______________ the gender of an unborn baby with a sonogram.

5. The stream came down from the long and narrow mountain ______________.

6. The police were forced to close off the roads that had been ______________ by heavy rainfall.

[7-12] Choose the words that are closest in meaning to the underlined ones.

7. Fans of the strange and unusual proposed some <u>outlandish</u> theories regarding the origin of the pyramids.

a. outrageous b. thoughtful c. rigid d. boring

8. Amy <u>possesses</u> rare talent as a writer and should pursue a future as an author.

a. appreciates b. has c. develops d. outgrows

9. The committee <u>dismissed</u> several of the theories for lack of evidence.

a. imitated b. improved c. forgot d. rejected

10. Slowly, the sugar coating <u>hardened</u> into a crisp, glass-like shell around the apple.

a. solidified b. formed c. sweetened d. stuck

11. The experiment <u>demonstrated</u> that cloning is indeed possible.

a. collaborated b. theorized c. questioned d. showed

12. Jefferson <u>formalized</u> his draft of the Declaration of Independence with the help of a committee.

a. shared b. scrapped c. started d. finalized

[13-15] Complete each sentence with the following idioms.

break apart / account for / due to

13. This coffee company ___________________ about 40% of the domestic coffee market.

14. A chunk of ice fell from the ice shelf and ______________ into numerous smaller pieces.

15. The prime minister was unable to attend the conference ___________________ a cold.

Reading Comprehension

1 What is the passage mainly about?

a. The most famous debate in the field of geology
b. How geologists arrived at the ideas behind the plate tectonics theory
c. Alfred Wegener's contributions to the theory of plate tectonics
d. What fossil evidence can tell us about the history of Earth

2 Which idea do the theories of continental drift and plate tectonics have in common?

a. Mid-ocean ridges are responsible for creating new earth.
b. Both continents and oceans rest atop moving plates.
c. Pangaea was the first manifestation of a supercontinent.
d. The positions of Earth's landmasses are not fixed.

3 What happens when two continental plates collide?

a. They break apart and move away from each other.
b. The fossils within them are dispersed.
c. Land is pushed up to create mountains.
d. New land is formed from cooling magma.

4 The word plausible in the passage is closest in meaning to

a. possible　　b. identical
c. beneficial　　d. simple

5 Which of the following was NOT part of Wegener's evidence in support of continental drift?

a. Underwater maps created by marine sonar technology
b. Geological correlations among disparate rock samples
c. Similarities in the shapes of coastlines
d. Remains of tropical life in Antarctica

6 What can be inferred about Antarctica?

a. There is a mid-ocean ridge near it.
b. It is the last remaining fragment of Pangaea.
c. It was once positioned close to the equator.
d. South America used to be attached directly to it.

7 What first made people consider the idea that the continents might be moving?

8 What do eastern South America and western Africa have in common?

9 What happens at a mid-ocean ridge?

Summary

Step 1 **Read the passage again and complete the outline with the words below.**

similarities / fossil / evidence / Pangaea / moving / Wegener's
plate tectonics / hypothesized / moving / continental drift / ridges

I. Earth's continents are constantly ____________

A. First suggested by thinkers who noted ____________ among coastlines

II. Alfred Wegener's work

A. ____________ about a past supercontinent called ____________

B. Collected rock and ____________ evidence to support his idea

C. Introduced a theory of ____________

D. His theory was rejected for lack of ____________

III. The theory of ____________

A. New sonar maps enabled the discovery of mid-ocean ____________

B. Earth's surface is made up of multiple ____________ plates

C. Finally proved ____________ theory correct

Step 2 **Complete the summary with your own words based on the outline.**

Throughout Earth's history, the continents have been constantly ________. ________
____
____
____
____
____
____
____ The theory of plate tectonics finally proved Wegener's theory of ____________ correct.

Unit 4: Dance Language Among Honey Bees

Getting Started

1. Look at the picture. What do you know about bees?
2. What are some of the ways humans communicate with one another?
3. Can you name any forms of animal communication?

Building Background Knowledge

Honeybees

Honeybees are bees that produce and store honey in nests made out of wax. They live in colonies of up to hundreds of thousands of bees. Each colony has one queen bee and a few to several thousand male bees, called drones, which exist only to mate with the queen. About 95 percent of the bees in a colony are female worker bees, and they live one to four months long during non-honey-making season. In the spring and summer when honey is made, female worker bees only live a few weeks.

The majority of the worker bees collect a sweet liquid called "nectar" from flower blossoms and bring it back to the colony. They mix the nectar with their saliva, which contains special chemicals that cause the nectar to turn into honey. This mixture of ingredients is stored in a beeswax comb where it is fanned with the wings of the worker bees to help evaporate the water. Then, the beeswax combs are closed off with wax and stored for the winter for eating.

UNIT 4

Dance Language Among Honey Bees

05

The Big Question

How are honey bees able to communicate with each other?

► Notes

Honey bees interact in ways more complex than we might imagine. Since ancient times, scientists have been aware that peculiar, dance-like movements are enacted by **forager** bees returning to the hive after locating a food source. It was assumed these "dances" were performed to draw the attention of other foragers and recruit their assistance in collecting **pollen**.

In 1947, however, a zoology professor named Karl von Frisch discovered a more intricate meaning behind the dances. He set up food sources near an **artificial** glass-walled hive and trained a group of foragers, marked with colored paint, to locate a source and return a pollen sample to the hive. Through careful observation of the bees' movements once inside, he **discerned** that, in addition to recruiting aid, the foragers' dances were providing specific data regarding the distance and direction of the food source. Moreover, the bees executed different dances depending on the type of information they needed to **convey**.

For instance, when a food **source** is close to the hive, relatively simple dances are performed. The forager completes a "round dance," running in tight little circles, for sources within 50 meters of the hive. A similar dance, called the "sickle dance," is utilized to advertise food sources between 50 and 150 meters away. Instead of a circular route, a bee performing the sickle dance follows a crescent-shaped path. Neither round nor sickle dances communicate anything concerning the direction in which the **sustenance** can be found.

When a honey bee has located a food source that lies more than 150

forager one who wanders in search of food
pollen powdery yellow substance on flowers containing male reproductive cells
artificial man-made; not found in nature
discern to recognize or understand
convey to pass from one place to another

meters away, it implements a "**waggle** dance." First, the forager runs forward in a straight line, vibrating its body so its back section appears to wag. It then **loops** outward in a semicircle to return to the starting point, after which it moves forward again in the same fashion and semicircles back on the opposite side. The distance of the forager's run during the waggle dance is proportional to the distance of the food source—the longer the run, the farther the pollen. In addition, the angle of the run describes the direction of the source, explaining its location in relation to the position of the sun. For example, if the pollen is located toward the sun, the forager traces a vertical line directly up the hive wall. If the pollen is located in the opposite direction from the sun, the forager runs straight down the wall. Otherwise, the angle of the pollen's location relative to the sun is reflected in the angle of the waggle run.

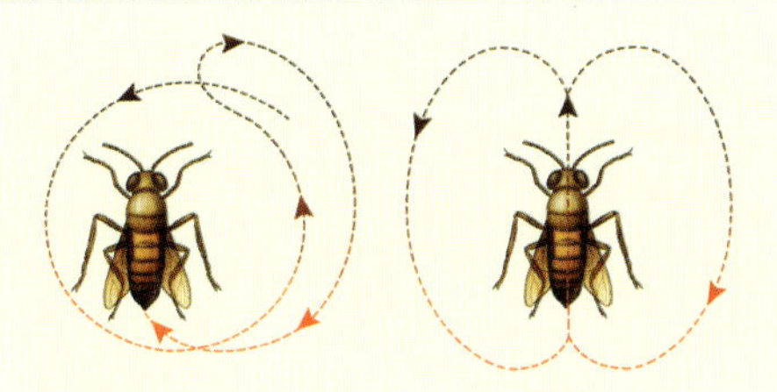

Figure 1. *Round dance*

Figure 2. *Waggle dance*

Von Frisch's dance language theory is often disputed; there are zoologists who argue foragers' movements are intended only to attract the attention of other bees. Instead, they believe **olfactory** data from the initial pollen sample found by the forager is enough to transmit the source's location. Even supporters of the dance language theory acknowledge the importance of smell. In fact, they feel that, although foragers' communicative dances can guide bees to the vicinity of a pollen store, olfactory clues are used to pinpoint the exact source.

▸ Notes

On Your Own

Have you ever witnessed animal communication? What animal was it, and how did it communicate?

source a place from which something arises
sustenance food that people or animals need in order to live
waggle to rock from side to side or back and forth
loop to move on a circular path
olfactory relating to the sense of smell

Vocabulary Building

[1-6] Complete each sentence with one of the words from the box.

intricate / vicinity / acknowledge / dispute / concerning / recruit

1. The ____________ design work must have been done by a master craftsperson.

2. The team said they would ____________ the referee's unfair call in court.

3. The recent investigation yielded no new information ____________ the ancient eruption.

4. I will admit to my mistakes if you will also ____________ yours.

5. People who lived in the ____________ of the test site have an increased risk of cancer.

6. The guild must ____________ a new gamer to fill the empty position.

[7-12] Choose the words that are closest in meaning to the underlined ones.

7. The community is struggling because it lacks the ability to <u>utilize</u> its resources.

a. protect b. encounter c. use d. distribute

8. Life vests are <u>located</u> beneath your chairs in case of an emergency.

a. situated b. received c. visited d. clued in

9. This <u>peculiar</u> moon is the only large moon that orbits backwards.

a. familiar b. favorable c. chilly d. distinctive

10. Archaeologists once <u>assumed</u> invaders destroyed the city but now wonder if the residents of the city did it themselves.

a. presumed b. allowed c. defeated d. noted

11. The gymnast will win first place because he <u>executed</u> his routine perfectly.

a. learned b. performed c. entertained d. described

12. Neurons <u>transmit</u> information to the brain with electrochemical signals.

a. process b. produce c. convey d. decode

[13-15] Complete each sentence with the following idioms.

in addition to / draw the attention of / in relation to

13. We serve vegetarian dishes ________________ meat dishes.

14. The colorful designs in the center of the flower help ________________ passing pollinators, like bees and birds.

15. The study compared mortality rates ________________ individuals' smoking habits.

Reading Comprehension

1 What is the main idea of the passage?

a. Honey bees have evolved different types of communicative dances over time.
b. Foragers are the only class of honey bee that is able to communicate.
c. Evidence supporting the honey bee dance language theory is nearly undeniable.
d. Honey bees convey information about food through dance movements.

2 How does the waggle dance differ from the round and sickle dances?

a. It only involves straight-line movement.
b. It is performed by multiple bees at once.
c. It transmits data on a food source's direction.
d. It is used only for particularly rich pollen stores.

3 Prior to 1947, what purpose were honey bee dances believed to serve?

a. to encourage other bees to help gather food
b. to attract potential mates for the forager
c. to illustrate the distance of various food sources
d. to explain that a bee had returned with pollen

4 The word intended in the passage is closest in meaning to

a. utilized
b. meant
c. shown
d. proposed

5 Which movement is NOT featured in a dance performed by forager bees?

a. A semicircular loop
b. A series of small circles
c. A crescent-shaped run
d. A short, circular flight

6 What can be inferred about the waggle dance?

a. It can be used at nighttime as well as during the day.
b. It was the last of the three dances to be studied.
c. It is named for the vibration displayed by the performer.
d. It is sometimes danced on the exterior of the beehive.

7 What do both opponents and supporters of the dance language theory agree on?

8 How did von Frisch research his dance language theory?

9 How is information communicated through the waggle dance?

Summary

Step 1 **Read the passage again and complete the outline with the words below.**

round / waggle / opponents / pollen / food
communication / movements / agree / sickle / smell

I. Honey bees' dance ____________

A. Originally thought to recruit other bees to help gather ____________

B. Studied and theorized as a method of ____________ by von Frisch

II. Specific dances that give information about ____________ sources

A. ____________ dance used for sources less than 50 meters from the hive

B. ____________ dance used for sources between 50 and 150 meters away

C. ____________ dance describes both distance and direction of faraway sources

III. ____________ of the dance language theory

A. Argue that bees can find food solely by ____________

B. Supporters of the theory ____________ that smell probably plays a role

Step 2 **Complete the summary with your own words based on the outline.**

For centuries, the dance movements of forager bees were thought to serve to recruit other bees to help gather ____________. However, ______________________

____

____

____

____

____

____

____ Supporters of the theory ____________ with this in part, feeling that smell probably does play some role.

Unit 5: The Invention of the Modern Printing Press

Getting Started

1 Look at the two images. How do you think they were made? What is different or similar about them?

2 What are some common book subjects that you might find in a bookstore?

3 How much does a novel cost in your country? What about a school textbook?

Building Background Knowledge

Printing Press

The world's very first printed book, *the Diamond Sutra*, was produced in China in 868 A.D. It was printed from woodblocks, which were an early form of printing technology made by carving letters into wooden blocks, dipping the blocks into ink, and then pressing them onto paper. Although this process for printing books was labor intensive, it was still more efficient than writing copies of books by hand. Even after book-printing technology emerged, books remained quite rare, as only about five copies of each book were made per year. Books (and reading in general) were reserved for church and government officials, and naturally, the earliest printed materials were primarily religious books and documents. The invention of the printing press changed that by making books cheaper and more accessible than ever before. Common people no longer had to depend so heavily on the church and government for ideas and information.

▲ Workers in a printing press

UNIT 5

The Invention of the Modern Printing Press

06

The Big Question

Why was Gutenberg's printing press so revolutionary?

▸ Notes

Prior to the 1300s, books were a scarce **commodity** in Europe. Each new copy of a text needed to be tediously copied from an earlier edition by hand. The workers charged with producing books were called scribes, and it often took a single **scribe** over a year to complete just one book. The extensive labor involved, coupled with the fact that book pages were made out of vellum—carefully treated and stretched animal skin—ensured that only the richest medieval Europeans could afford to own a book. Yet, at this time, the continent was slowly beginning to emerge from the **Dark Ages**. General wealth and **literacy rates** were rising, culminating in a heightened demand for books.

Bookmakers of the 1300s and early 1400s sought to meet this demand by adopting printing technologies from Asia. The most notable was a Chinese technique known as woodblock printing. A word, a sentence, or an entire page was carved into a block of wood, ink was applied to the surface, and the block was pressed onto a sheet of vellum, cloth, or paper. While woodblock printing eliminated the need for text to be handwritten, it failed to increase the production of books in any dramatic fashion. The woodblocks were very delicate, cracking easily, and the **carvings** faded quickly. Moreover, the time it took to create the carvings was still substantial.

In the 1430s, a **metalsmith** named Johannes Gutenberg began work on an improved printing press. In place of woodblocks, he employed metal moveable type, a technology that had been invented centuries earlier in

commodity a product or substance that is sold or bought
scribe one who makes copies of books for a profession
Dark Ages the period of European history from 476 A.D. to 1000 A.D.
literacy rate the percentage of the population that can read and write
carving a design engraved into a surface

► Notes

Korea but gone underutilized. Using a durable **alloy** mixture, he fashioned small metal stamps for each of the 26 letters of the Latin alphabet. These stamps could be placed in whatever arrangement was needed to print one page of a book and then rearranged to print the next one. The ease of arranging the moveable type compared to carving a block of wood greatly reduced the effort involved in book printing. Working with this press, a single person could now produce hundreds of copies of a book per year. Gutenberg also **pioneered** the use of longer-lasting oil-based inks and printed on low-cost paper in addition to vellum.

▲ Gutenberg Printing Press

The impact of Gutenberg's invention on European society became evident immediately. Before the close of the century, thousands of printers were in business, mass-producing hundreds of thousands of books. Prices plummeted, giving ordinary people access to written texts for the first time in history. Whereas previously books had dealt primarily with **religious** matters, these new books covered a greater variety of subjects, and different European **vernaculars** were featured alongside the standard Latin. Philosophical and scientific ideas from ancient Greece and Rome, as well as discoveries being made by contemporary thinkers, were rapidly diffused throughout the continent. Seen in this light, the printing press can be understood as one of the most important factors propelling Europe into the Renaissance in the 16th century, a period that ushered in the modern age.

▲ Medieval scribe

On Your Own

Do you prefer to write by hand or type on a computer?

metalsmith one who works with metal
alloy a metal made by mixing two or more metals
pioneer to prepare the way for and help introduce
religious relating to religion in general or to a particular religion
vernacular the language or dialect of a certain region

Vocabulary Building

[1-6] Complete each sentence with one of the words from the box.

contemporary / tediously / substantial / delicate / cover / evident

1. The geometrical style was used by the Dipylon Master and ____________ Greek potters.

2. The photographer ____________ labeled thousands of photographs by hand.

3. The scientist's discoveries have led to ____________ advances in many fields.

4. The fine antiques are too ____________ to be moved or used on a daily basis.

5. The documentary will ____________ Al Gore's entire political career.

6. It was ____________ that she was smart based on her good grades.

[7-12] Choose the words that are closest in meaning to the underlined ones.

7. I got mad when the editor asked me to make extensive revisions to my novel.
a. respectful b. constructive c. careful d. lengthy

8. The most notable of the plague outbreaks occurred in the 14th century.
a. deadly b. arguable c. important d. widely studied

9. The president promised to completely eliminate the budget deficit by next year.
a. assess b. prevent c. decrease d. get rid of

10. Buddhism originated in ancient India but diffused throughout Asia and the West.
a. spread b. pledged c. assembled d. evolved

11. My dad fashioned a solar oven out of materials he found around the house.
a. presented b. made c. chose d. favored

12. Catapults were employed by medieval armies to attack walled cities.
a. discouraged b. constructed c. admitted d. utilized

[13-15] Complete each sentence with the following idioms.

in place of / usher in / deal with

13. The article ________________ the effects of second-hand smoke on young children.

14. The new trade route ________________ an era of prosperity for Singapore.

15. In case don't have any eggs, applesauce may be used ________________ them.

Reading Comprehension

1 What is the passage mainly about?

a. the development of a printing technology in Europe
b. the development of new printing methods in medieval times
c. how the modern printing press changed European society
d. differences between the modern printing press and earlier devices

2 How were books printed in Europe during the Dark Ages?

a. by employing metal moveable type
b. with small wooden stamps of the alphabet
c. with full-page woodblock carvings
d. by copying text one word at a time

3 Which earlier technology most closely resembled Gutenberg's printing press?

a. metal moveable type from Korea
b. a press popularized by the Greeks and the Romans
c. oil-based inks developed during the Dark Ages
d. woodblock printing from China

4 The word culminating in the passage is closest in meaning to

a. resulting b. accepting
c. entering d. following

5 Which of the following is NOT a reason why woodblocks failed to increase book production?

a. The wood was expensive to acquire.
b. The carvings on the blocks wore down quickly.
c. They required a great deal of time to produce.
d. The wood was fragile and easily broken.

6 What can be inferred about European books printed before the 1430s?

a. They were produced using cheap vellum.
b. They reached a wide audience.
c. They generally included text in Latin.
d. They covered topics like literature and science.

7 What were two factors that made books unaffordable to all but the wealthiest medieval Europeans?

8 What were the primary components of Gutenberg's printing press?

9 What effect did the mass production of books have on Europe?

Summary

Step 1 **Read the passage again and complete the outline with the words below.**

books / woodblock / impact / carve / metal / stamps / Dark Ages / scribes
printing press / Chinese / mass production / religion / Renaissance

I. ______________ in Europe before the 1300s

A. Scarce and expensive, copied by ______________

B. Demand rose after ______________

II. Adoption of ______________ technology

A. ______________ woodblock technique eliminated the need for scribes

B. Blocks were delicate and hard to ______________, book production did not increase

III. Gutenberg's improved ______________

A. Based on ______________ moveable type

B. Used metal ______________ for each letter, could be rearranged

IV. ______________ of the printing press

A. ______________ gave public access to books

B. Subject matter shifted from ______________ to science and philosophy

C. Helped lead Europe into the ______________

Step 2 **Complete the summary with your own words based on the outline.**

Before the 1300s, __________ in Europe were scarce and expensive, since each text had to be hand-copied by ______________. ____

____

____

____

____

____

__________ Eventually, the printing press helped lead Europe into the ______________.

Part II

• Content Area : History

Unit 6: Decoding the Rosetta Stone

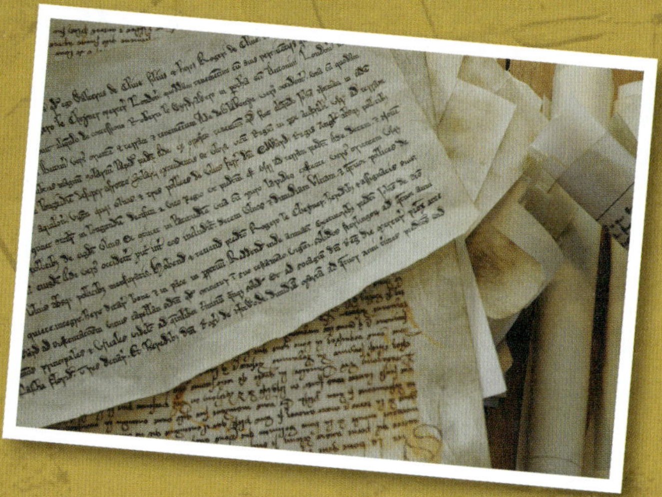

Getting Started

1. Why do we have systems for writing down spoken languages?
2. What is the main language spoken in your country? What is the meaning of your name in your national language?
3. Can you guess what ancient letters might have looked like?

Building Background Knowledge

Egyptian Hieroglyphs

Hieroglyphs are sacred drawings that were used by the Egyptians from around 3000 B.C. to 400 A.D. Originally, the Egyptians drew pictures to represent letters, things, and ideas. But then, the Greeks conquered Egypt, and under Alexander the Great, the Egyptians started using the Greek alphabet. They continued to use hieroglyphs for things related to religion until 400 A.D., when they stopped using them altogether because most people converted to Christianity.

Hieroglyphs were simple drawings of everyday objects such as animals, houses, or trees. To write the word "dog," the Egyptians drew a picture of a dog. If they wanted to write about five dogs, they would draw one picture of a dog and then five lines next to it. Later on, they began combining pictures to make new words. For example, the sound of one word plus the sound of another word could be placed side by side to make the sound of something else altogether.

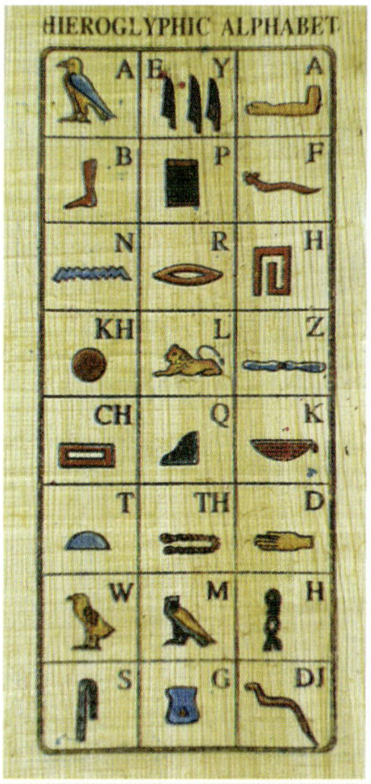

▲ Hieroglyphic alphabet

UNIT 6

The Big Question

Why was the discovery of the Rosetta Stone so important?

Decoding the Rosetta Stone

07

▸ Notes

The ancient Egyptian system of writing was among the world's earliest forms of written communication. It originally developed as a collection of pictographs, or hieroglyphs, which are symbols that were drawn to represent specific objects or ideas. However, over the centuries these symbols evolved to stand for spoken sounds, like the letters of the English alphabet. Hieroglyphs were sometimes written on papyrus scrolls, an early manifestation of paper made from dried reeds, but they appeared most often **etched** into the stone walls of temple buildings. The writing system was therefore given the name hieroglyphics, which means '**sacred** writing.'

Unfortunately, sometime around 400 A.D. the use of hieroglyphics ceased, and with it vanished all knowledge of how to read this script. Even during times when hieroglyphic writing was most prominent, at the height of the ancient Egyptian civilization, very few people could interpret the characters. Reading and writing were skills reserved for scribes and government officials in charge of taxation and other administrative tasks. Therefore, it did not take long for proficiency in hieroglyphics to fade once the system was no longer employed by the Egyptian government, and the secrets of the hieroglyphs remained a mystery until the 1799 discovery of an **artifact** called the Rosetta Stone.

French soldiers in Napoleon's army, which had launched an invasion of Egypt, found the stone while digging the foundations of a fort near el-Rashid, also known as Rosetta. The object was a large slab of rock 45 inches long by 28 inches wide, and it featured three **inscriptions** in

etch to cut a design into a surface
sacred endowed with spiritual or religious importance
artifact an historically valuable item from the past
inscription text carved into a hard surface
commoner a person who has no title of nobility

three different languages: hieroglyphics, Demotic, and Greek. Demotic was the script used by Egyptian **commoners** at the time of the stone's construction, around 196 B.C., and Greek was the language of government. The inscriptions told of a royal **decree** passed down by a council of priests, but more importantly, each inscription said the same thing. Thus, scholars assumed they would be able to pair the hieroglyphs to the well-known Greek characters and uncover the meanings and **syntax** of the ancient writing system.

Many accomplished linguists attempted to **decipher** the Rosetta Stone, but it was not until 1822 that one succeeded. His name was Jean-Francois Champollion, a French classical scholar, and though he benefited greatly from the contributions of others, he claimed total credit for decoding the hieroglyphic system. His breakthrough came with the realization that the hieroglyphs were not merely pictorial but possessed **phonetic** values, much like a modern alphabet.

▲ Rosetta Stone

The impact of Champollion's achievement is difficult to measure, but it is safe to say that nearly all we now know about ancient Egypt's history, myths, society, and beliefs was made possible by the decoding of the Rosetta Stone. Once the code was cracked, scholars went out to the region's plentiful **archaeological** sites and began translating as much "sacred writing" as they could. Indeed, this was the birth of a new field of study called Egyptology, which has since given us a vastly greater understanding of human history and the lives of our ancestors.

▸ Notes

On Your Own

Have you ever made your own "secret" code? When did you use it, and why?

decree an order from an authority
syntax the appropriate order of words in sentences and phrases
decipher to figure out the meaning of something
phonetic relating to the sounds produced when speaking
archaeological relating to the study of historic cultures through their remains

Vocabulary Building

[1-6] Complete each sentence with one of the words from the box.

breakthrough / plentiful / specific / fade / represent / benefit

1. Though it was discovered long ago, no one knows what the Zbruch Idol might ____________.

2. I'm looking for a ____________ brand of sewing machine that comes from Germany.

3. At the end of the play, the lights ____________ and the curtain falls.

4. Wild boars live longer when food is ____________ than when it is scare.

5. Researchers made a medical ____________ that could reduce the global impact of malaria.

6. Residents of coastal communities stand to ____________ from the wave farm project.

[7-12] Choose the words that are closest in meaning to the underlined ones.

7. The truck driver had <u>vanished</u> without a trace, leaving the police no leads to pursue.
a. announced b. departed c. worked d. disappeared

8. Angered by his harsh words, Mary <u>ceased</u> being sweet to him.
a. struggled b. stopped c. expired d. counted

9. A research team announced they had <u>uncovered</u> clues to the origin of ovarian cancer.
a. followed b. examined c. reported d. found

10. Scientists are trying to <u>decode</u> the structure of human genes.
a. declare b. interpret c. correspond d. conceal

11. Her <u>proficiency</u> as a programmer made her invaluable to the company.
a. skill b. attitude c. experience d. education

12. Curie received Nobel Prizes for her <u>achievements</u> in both physics and chemistry.
a. rewards b. aggression c. passion d. accomplishments

[13-15] Complete each sentence with the following idioms.

stand for / be safe to say / claim credit for

13. They found initials carved into the tree and wondered what they ____________.

14. No one wanted to help me but everyone wants to ____________ my success.

15. I don't know if he's a genius, but I think it ____________ that he is very smart.

Reading Comprehension

1 What is the passage mainly about?

a. the Egyptian writing system and the decoding of the Rosetta Stone
b. the life and work of the French scholar Jean-Francois Champollion
c. the development, evolution, and uses of Egyptian hieroglyphs
d. the historic importance and role of ancient Egyptian civilization

2 How did hieroglyphs evolve over time?

a. They became symbols representing objects and ideas.
b. They started to function as individual letters.
c. They transformed from an alphabet into pictographs.
d. They gradually became simpler in form.

3 Why did the ability to interpret hieroglyphs fade so quickly?

a. Use of the script was outlawed by government officials.
b. Few people knew how to read and write the characters.
c. The script was written on impermanent materials, like papyrus.
d. A foreign army invaded Egypt shortly after 400 A.D.

4 The word cracked in the passage is closest in meaning to

a. solved b. initiated
c. accepted d. heard

5 Which of the following is NOT true about the Rosetta Stone?

a. It was unearthed by Napoleon's army when they invaded Egypt.
b. It was not translated until more than 20 years after its discovery.
c. It was inscribed with two language systems: hieroglyphs and Greek.
d. It featured a royal decree delivered by a council of priests.

6 What can be inferred about the hieroglyphic writing system?

a. Knowledge about it was intentionally kept secret.
b. Scribes stopped using it around 400 A.D.
c. It had much in common with the Greek writing system.
d. It was designed for commoners who couldn't read Greek.

7 What does the word "hieroglyphics" mean, and why is it an appropriate term for the ancient Egyptian system of writing?

8 What did the Rosetta Stone look like?

9 How did scholars use the Greek characters to decode the Rosetta Stone?

Summary

Step 1 **Read the passage again and complete the outline with the words below.**

hieroglyphic / Rosetta Stone / writing / two / decoded / current / earliest
vanished / Napoleon's army / Champollion's translation / scribes / government

I. The ancient Egyptian ____________ system

A. One of the ____________ forms of written communication

B. Made up of pictographs, or hieroglyphics, that represented spoken sounds

II. Extinction of the ____________ writing system

A. ____________ from use sometime around 400 A.D.

B. Had only been known to ____________ and ____________ officials

III. The discovery of the ____________

A. Found by ____________

B. Contained translations of hieroglyphs into ____________ other writing systems

IV. ____________ of the Rosetta Stone

A. Successfully ____________ the hieroglyphic system

B. Greatly contributed to ____________ understanding of ancient Egypt

Step 2 **Complete the summary with your own words based on the outline.**

The ________ system of ancient Egypt was one of the ____________ forms of written communication. ____

____

____

____

____

____________________ His work greatly contributed to our ____________ understanding of ancient Egypt and led to the foundation of the field of Egyptology.

Unit 7: The Great Depression

Getting Started

1. Do you know what it means to be depressed? How does a depressed person feel?
2. What might cause a person or group of people to be depressed?
3. Have you ever heard of the stock market? What is it and how does it work?

Building Background Knowledge

Black Tuesday

The Great Depression began in the U.S. on October 29, 1929, when the stock market suddenly crashed. The losses from that entire week totaled $30 billion, which would be equal to $377,587,032,770.41 today.

The day the stock market crashed was so grim that people named it "Black Tuesday." The value of the stock market continued to shrink for several years after Black Tuesday, as well. The stock market's value, which had been at 386.10 in September of 1929, reached an all-time low in July of 1932, when it fell to 40.60. In less than three years, the stock market had lost a total of 89 percent of its value.

The majority of people who had invested money in the stock market lost their savings. The stock market crash also caused many banks to close, which in turn led to more people losing money. The effects of the Great Depression were so astounding that they lasted until the early 1940s and could be felt around the entire world.

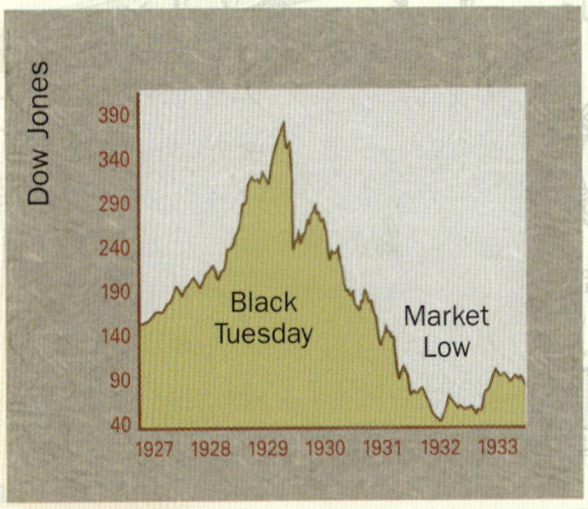

▲ Dow Jones: an indicator of stock market prices based on share values

UNIT 7

The Big Question

What characterized the period of the Great Depression in the United States?

The Great Depression

08

▸ Notes

The world's economies had experienced economic **recessions** and even depressions many times in the decades prior to 1929. However, none had reached the **severity**, in terms of both financial loss and duration, of that experienced during the 1930s, a period now known as the Great Depression. Many nations felt its effects, but few suffered as extensively as the United States. In America, thousands of banks and businesses failed, and unemployment and homelessness prevailed into the early 1940s.

While the exact combination of financial and social factors that caused the Great Depression will likely never be fully understood, one event is recognized as its initial manifestation: the U.S. stock market crash of late October, 1929. As stock values plummeted, investors panicked and sold their **shares** at a loss, **crippling** entire companies in the process. Average Americans, worried about access to their **savings**, made massive **withdrawals**, which in turn led to a series of bank collapses. **Funds** evaporated, employers could not afford to compensate their workers, and farmers and homeowners became unable to pay their **mortgages**. Widespread homelessness and unemployment was the result, with the latter reaching a figure of 25% by 1932.

The American leader presiding over this financial disaster was Herbert Hoover. Following a philosophy of limited government, he refused to take federal action to stem the collapse, believing the market would correct itself. Needless to say, the millions of Americans living without work or shelter did not support this tactic. So it was not unexpected when, in the

recession a period of economic slowdown
severity harshness or hardness
share a fraction of the ownership of a company
cripple to weaken or damage seriously
savings a quantity of money saved, especially in a bank account

elections of 1932, Hoover was overwhelmingly defeated by challenger Franklin Roosevelt, who promised decisive government action to end the Depression.

Roosevelt immediately **instituted** a bundle of policies he termed the New Deal, aimed at righting the U.S. economy through **federal** intervention. He placed a temporary ban on bank withdrawals to prevent more bank failures and passed laws to support the recovery of businesses. He distributed money to families for food and clothing purchases, implemented a program of unemployment compensation, and founded the Social Security system to provide financial assistance to the elderly. Moreover, the New Deal created numerous government agencies to generate employment. These included the Civilian Conservation Corps, which hired workers to replant deforested areas; the Works Progress Administration, which created jobs in construction as well as among artists; and the Tennessee Valley Authority, which extended electricity service to rural communities through hydroelectric projects.

▲ Statues of unemployed men standing in an unemployment line during the Great Depression at the FDR Memorial in Washington, D.C.

Despite the breadth of the New Deal policies, they were more successful in halting the Depression than reversing it. It was not until America's soldiers and, consequently, its industries became engaged in World War II that true recovery occurred. However, many of Roosevelt's programs, such as unemployment compensation and Social Security, remain, and today they are considered fundamentals of American society. In addition, subsequent analyses of the causes and consequences of the Great Depression have informed federal policymakers on how to avoid future catastrophes. Ultimately, the Great Depression transformed perceptions about the role the federal government should play in economic matters.

▸ Notes

On Your Own

Do your parents create tasks for you so that you may earn an allowance?

withdrawal the act of taking out money from a bank account
funds a supply of currency available for use
mortgage a loan used to purchase property
institute to put in place or set up
federal relating to the central government of a nation

Vocabulary Building

[1-6] Complete each sentence with one of the words from the box.

afford / collapse / compensate / evaporate / widespread / intervention

1. The ______________ of the Soviet Union in 1991 brought the long Cold War to an end.

2. She knew his anger would ______________ when he saw the apology note and flowers.

3. Employers have started to ______________ underpaid employees with certain benefits.

4. A fictional radio drama caused ______________ panic when it said Martians had invaded.

5. Parents seek government ______________ in the fight against child obesity.

6. Some financial analysts say the U.S. cannot ______________ to keep its space shuttles in operation.

[7-12] Choose the words that are closest in meaning to the underlined ones.

7. Gossip prevailed in the office, creating tension among workers.
a. abounded b. entered c. judged d. upset

8. Coffee prices have plummeted to an all-time low in recent years.
a. veered b. crashed c. leapt d. flapped

9. Supplies of food have arrived, but aid workers have no way to distribute them.
a. issue b. store c. purchase d. open

10. You should appy direct pressure to the wound to stem the flow of blood.
a. direct b. heal c. release d. stop

11. Hopefully, the fundraiser will generate enough money to sustain operations.
a. challenge b. fix c. create d. enclose

12. Several major actions were taken to halt the spread of AIDS in Africa.
a. displace b. encourage c. ponder d. cease

[13-15] Complete each sentence with the following idioms.

needless to say / prior to / place a ban on

13. It is polite to call ______________ visiting.

14. I threw up on the table on our first date; ______________, we didn't meet again.

15. The city has ______________ street parking, so you might have to move your car.

Reading Comprehension

1 What is the passage mainly about?

a. the effects of and recovery from the Great Depression
b. differences between Hoover's and Roosevelt's administrations
c. financial and social conditions that led to the Great Depression
d. how the U.S. government once dealt with economic difficulties

2 What was the major difference between Hoover's and Roosevelt's approaches to the Great Depression?

a. Only Hoover discouraged people from withdrawing from their bank accounts.
b. Hoover was more certain about the potential economic benefits of going to war.
c. Hoover focused on unemployment, while Roosevelt addressed homelessness.
d. Roosevelt created new regulations, while Hoover waited for the market to heal itself.

3 What event signaled the start of the Great Depression?

a. the global spread of social problems before the 1920s
b. the crash of the U.S. stock market in 1929
c. the rapid rise in unemployment among Americans
d. the series of bank failures in the late 1920s

4 The word perceptions in the passage is closest in meaning to

a. regulations b. arguments
c. viewpoints d. questions

5 Which of the following is NOT mentioned as a provision of Roosevelt's New Deal?

a. It provided financial compensation to the unemployed.
b. It prohibited people from accessing their savings.
c. It created a system of shelters to house the homeless.
d. It generated new jobs in construction and conservation.

6 What can be inferred about Herbert Hoover's philosophy of limited government?

a. It enabled Hoover to delay the U.S. entry into World War II.
b. It failed to produce solutions to help the troubled economy.
c. It allowed the market sufficient time to correct itself.
d. It resulted in the worst stock market crash in history.

7 What reversed the Depression and led to economic recovery?

8 How did the Great Depression differ from previous economic depressions?

9 Which of Roosevelt's New Deal policies have survived?

Summary

Step 1 **Read the passage again and complete the outline with the words below.**

stock market / Roosevelt / job creation / New Deal / Hoover / World War II
severe / restricting / Depression / end / persisted / unemployment

I. The Great Depression of the 1930s

A. Longer and more ____________ than any previous depression

B. The ____________ crash of 1929 was the first major indication

C. Banks collapsed, ____________ soared, and homelessness rose

II. ____________ during the Depression

A. Believed in ____________ the government's involvement in the economy

B. His strategy was unpopular, was defeated by ____________

III. Roosevelt's handling of the ____________

A. Introduced the ____________, policies to help the economy and citizens

B. Social programs and ____________ slowed the Depression

IV. The ____________ of the Depression

A. ____________ engaged American industries and reversed the Depression

B. Certain New Deal policies ____________, becoming parts of U.S. society

Step 2 **Complete the summary with your own words based on the outline.**

The Great Depression of the 1930s was longer and more ____________ than any previous depression. ____

____

____

____

____

____ Since then, certain New Deal policies have ____________, becoming parts of U.S. society.

Unit 8: Understanding Hurricanes

Getting Started

1 Have you ever seen a hurricane on TV? What do you remember about it?

2 Do you know what the safety procedures are in case of a hurricane?

3 Besides hurricanes, what other natural disasters do you know about?

Building Background Knowledge

Hurricane Katrina

Hurricane Katrina, which occured during the hurricane season of 2005, was among the most devastating storms ever to hit the United States. Regarded as a mild threat when it first made landfall in Southern Florida, Katrina caused only minor flooding and loss of life in this region. However, it strengthened rapidly once it crossed into the warm waters of the Gulf of Mexico. The storm slammed into the southern coast of Louisiana and caused enormous damage throughout the state, largely due to the storm surge, or sudden rise in water level, that accompanied it.

The levee system designed to protect low-lying New Orleans failed, and the city and surrounding parishes were submerged under several feet of water. The flood waters lingered for weeks, leaving many local residents stranded without access to food, medical supplies, or fresh water. In all, Hurricane Katrina led to over 1,800 casualties, a statistic which makes it the deadliest tropical storm in the U.S. since 1928.

▲ Flooded area of New Orleans following Hurricane Katrina

UNIT 8

The Big Question

What factor drives the creation and growth of hurricanes?

Understanding Hurricanes

► Notes

The most destructive type of storm on Earth, producing devastating winds and **torrential** rain, is the hurricane, a word originating from the **extinct** Caribbean language of the Taíno people and their name for the god of storms, Juracán. When speaking more technically, **meteorologists** prefer the term "tropical cyclone," referring to both where the storm forms and its cyclical shape. In Asia, the **phenomenon** is known as a typhoon, but regardless of which **terminology** is used, hurricanes are defined as storms with **sustained** wind speeds of at least 74 miles per hour.

Hurricanes develop over open tropical oceans under certain conditions, the most significant of which involves water temperature; the ocean surface must be at or above 80 degrees Fahrenheit for a hurricane to form. This heat is transferred to the humid, tropical air above the water, pushing it upwards at great speeds and causing the moisture within it to build into tall clouds. As warm air vacates the lower altitudes, cooler air rushes in from all sides to take its place, resulting in strong winds. The winds begin to spin, a phenomenon generated by Earth's rotation, and a cyclonic storm is born.

The storm takes on a thick, ring-like structure with a hollow core known as the "eye," which is shaped like a narrow cylindrical **shaft**. Within the eye, there is little to no wind and the sky is clear of clouds, but directly surrounding it rise tall, dense thunderclouds where storm activity is the most

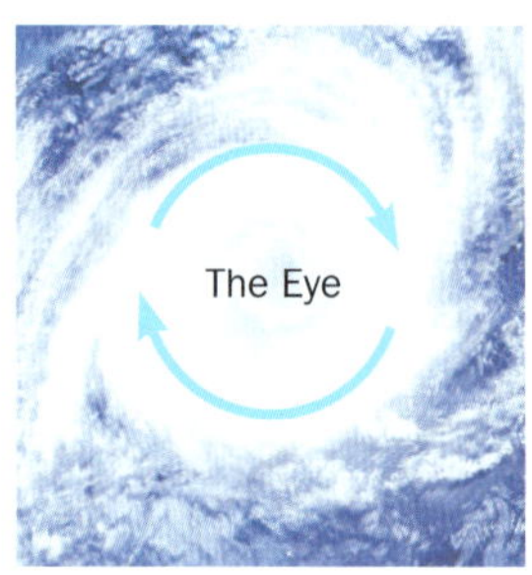

torrential occurring in large amounts and with great force
extinct no longer in existence
meteorologist a scientist who studies the weather
phenomenon an event in nature or society, especially something unusual
terminology the set of words used in a particular discipline

violent. This region is called the "eyewall," and depending on the overall girth of the storm, it may extend anywhere from 10 to 50 miles out from the eye. Beyond the eyewall, weaker storms known as "rain bands" orbit the eye, forming a giant **spiral** or wheel.

► Notes

As long as the storm remains over areas of warm water, its intensity increases; it can be thought of as "feeding" on this warmth. Once its winds reach sustained speeds of 38 miles per hour it is declared a tropical storm, and hurricane status is bestowed when the figure reaches 74 mph, but it can continue to climb to 185 mph and perhaps even higher. It will keep building in strength until it passes over cooler water or makes landfall.

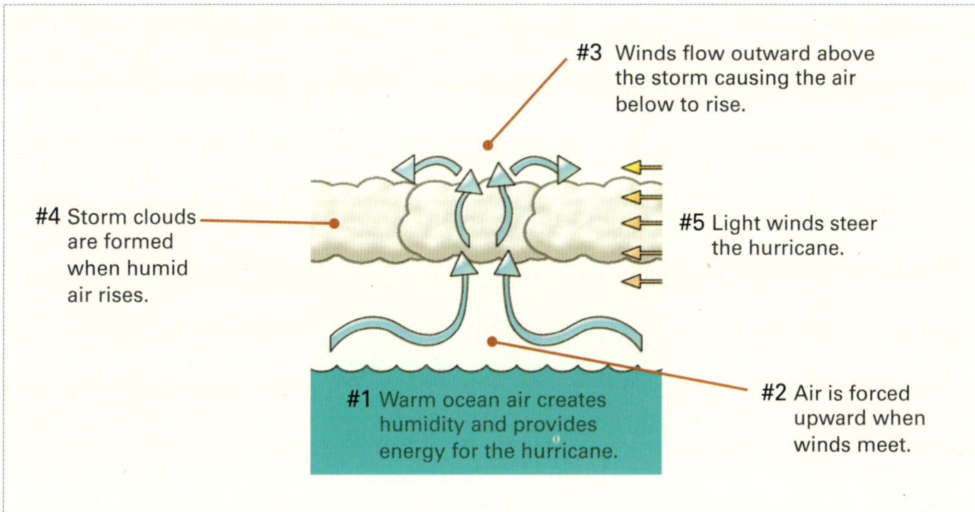

▲ How a hurricane is formed

Not surprisingly, hurricanes result in tremendous damage when they come ashore. Their winds are forceful enough to tear the roofs off of buildings, flip automobiles, and blow down power lines, and the rains they unleash can lead to severe flooding hundreds of miles inland. Hurricane winds also give rise to elevated sea levels that rush in as "storm surges" and flood entire coastal cities, and once on land, they can **spawn** separate but equally destructive thunderstorms and tornadoes. All told, a single hurricane may cause thousands of deaths and hundreds of millions of dollars in property damage. Like any natural disaster, hurricanes require ample preparation and a healthy dose of respect in order to minimize the harm they dispense.

On Your Own

Have you ever experienced a powerful storm? What was it like?

sustained occurring without slowing or stopping
shaft a long, narrow vertical passage
girth the measurement of the distance around something
spiral a shape made up of interconnected loops
spawn to make something happen or develop

Vocabulary Building

[1-6] Complete each sentence with one of the words from the box.

devastating / tremendous / flood / minimize / orbit / unleashed

1. The government abandoned its plan because of the ______________ opposition.
2. The spoiled child ______________ a terrible wail whenever someone told him no.
3. Much to her annoyance, the fly began to ______________ endlessly around her head.
4. In order to ______________ expenses, we only stayed in the cheapest hotels.
5. The terrible news had a(n) ______________ effect on the whole family.
6. Water from the broken pipe will quickly ______________ the basement.

[7-12] Choose the words that are closest in meaning to the underlined ones.

7. Because of the <u>dense</u> fog, the police decided to close down the highway.
   a. strict b. thick c. scattered d. thin

8. When the <u>violent</u> storm finally passed, the town was in a state of panic.
   a. influential b. mild c. complementary d. destructive

9. The king decided to <u>bestow</u> the title of duke to his childhood friend.
   a. award b. pass down c. create d. complain

10. The arm of the enormous crane <u>extended</u> outward across the skyline.
   a. shone b. disappeared c. shriveled d. reached

11. Given <u>ample</u> time, anyone would be able to solve such a problem.
   a. additional b. unreasonable c. little d. sufficient

12. The aid workers <u>dispensed</u> food and medicine to the earthquake victims.
   a. distributed b. relocated c. collected d. identified

[13-15] Complete each sentence with the following idioms.

result in / regardless of / not surprisingly

13. ____________________ your fear of heights, you need to climb up that ladder.
14. A simple change in diet could ____________________ a significant increase in energy.
15. ____________________, the most popular kid in school was elected class president.

Reading Comprehension

1 What is the passage mainly about?

a. methods for preventing damage during a hurricane
b. different ways of defining what a hurricane is
c. the formation and destructive potential of hurricanes
d. a description of the structure of the average hurricane

2 What do tropical storms and hurricanes have in common?

a. They cause thousands of deaths each year.
b. They may generate wind gusts of up to 185 mph.
c. They form only in the warm waters of the Caribbean.
d. They feature constant wind speeds of greater than 38 mph.

3 Where is the storm activity in a hurricane most intense?

a. within the clouds of the eyewall
b. less than 10 miles from the eye
c. at the center of the storm's eye
d. within the orbiting rain bands

4 The word vacates in the passage is closest in meaning to

a. heats
b. leaves
c. carries
d. bars

5 Which of the following is NOT a threat posed by hurricanes on land?

a. extremely low temperatures
b. the creation of tornadoes
c. coastal flooding due to storm surges
d. dangerously high wind speeds

6 What can be inferred about the Taíno people?

a. Their culture respected the power of hurricanes and other storms.
b. They devised a way of predicting the occurrence of hurricanes.
c. Their name for hurricanes was similar to that used today.
d. They experienced more hurricanes than any other culture.

7 How do hurricanes form?

8 Why do the winds of a cyclonic storm rotate?

9 What must happen for a hurricane to weaken?

Summary

Step 1 **Read the passage again and complete the outline with the words below.**

cool / formation / eye / warm / high / naming / threats / location
sustained / damage / cycle / stronger / property

I. ______________ hurricanes

A. Hurricanes have more than one name depending on their ______________.

B. All hurricanes are defined as having ______________ wind speeds above 74 mph

II. ______________ of hurricanes

A. ______________ ocean water pushes air upwards to form clouds

B. ______________ air blows in and creates ______________ winds, which rotate

III. ______________ of hurricanes

A. Made up of the ______________, eyewall, and rain bands

B. Grow ______________ over warm water, can reach wind speeds of 185 mph

IV. ______________ caused by hurricanes on land

A. Winds, rain, flooding, and tornadoes pose ______________

B. Many deaths and much ______________ damage result each year

Step 2 **Complete the summary with your own words based on the outline.**

Hurricanes have more than one name depending on their ______________. __________

____

____

____

____

____

____

Many deaths and much ______________ damage result from these storms each year.

Part II

Unit 9: What Are GMOs?

Getting Started

1. Have you heard the term GMO before? Can you guess what it stands for?
2. Look at the picture. What is it? Would you like to eat genetically modified food? Why or why not?
3. Name some foods available in your stores that come from abroad.

Building Background Knowledge

Risks of Genetic Modification

▲ GMO–Free Label

Genetically modified(GM) food is created by altering the DNA of an organism through complex biotechnological processes. These processes involve either the incorporation of selected genes from a completely different organism, or the recombination of the organism's existing genes.

Changes to a food's DNA can make it more resistant to insects and herbicides and give it a higher tolerance for environmental stress. Food can also be genetically modified to increase its nutritional value. However, there are concerns about the safety of GM crops. For the time being, there is not that much information on the potential health hazards of GM foods. Some experts worry that GM crops may create stronger bacteria that are resistant to antibiotics. They also fear that genetically modifying food may make it toxic or cause allergic reactions in consumers. Furthermore, there have been several reports of animals dying after having eaten a diet of GM foods.

UNIT 9

The Big Question

What is the definition of a genetically modified crop?

What Are GMOs? 10

► Notes

Would you eat a plant whose genes were altered by scientists in a laboratory? You probably already have, for genetically modified organisms (GMOs), also known as genetically engineered organisms, are widespread in modern food supplies. The concept underlying genetic modification is not new. For centuries, farmers have used a method called **selective breeding** to produce more **resilient** crops. They do this by choosing seeds from plants that appear to be particularly resistant to pests and cold or dry weather and planting those seeds in place of weaker **strains**. Over time, the desirable strains come to dominate the genetic **profiles** of the farmers' crops.

In the 1980s, scientists developed a shortcut to the time-intensive and unpredictable selective breeding process. Using advanced laboratory equipment, they learned how to insert genetic material directly into plant seeds, leading to the immediate adoption of desirable **characteristics** in the plants. These were the first GMOs. Additionally, the scientists discovered they could transfer genes from non-plant species, such as bacteria, to food crops. Currently, just over a dozen countries around the world produce and sell GMOs, with the United States responsible for the majority of the crops. Along with corn, soybeans are the most common genetically modified crop.

The advantages of GMOs are obvious. Farmers enjoy higher crop yields because fewer plants are lost to pests, **cold spells**, and **droughts**. Plants with pest-resistant genes also require fewer pesticide treatments, leading

selective breeding the process of breeding to achieve desirable traits

resilient able to become healthy or strong again quickly after suffering from misfortune

strain a genetically related group with specific traits

profile a description of a thing or person

characteristic a quality that distinguishes someone or something

▸ Notes

to safer **produce** for consumers and reducing the threat of environmental contamination. Moreover, many GMOs contain nutritious substances necessary to good health, as everything from vitamins to **pharmaceutical** drugs can be implanted in crop seeds, something that proponents of GMOs say could one day bring about the end of hunger in the developing world.

Not everyone is supportive of the technology, however. Critics point to the fact that GM foods are simply too new to be embraced, alleging that there could exist long-term health risks that have yet to surface. Also, consumers with allergies have had adverse reactions to the implanted genes; due to the lack of labels on GMOs, they did not realize they were ingesting something that could harm them. In response to claims that GM foods could help end hunger, critics say the seeds of these plants are patent-protected and much too expensive for farmers in poor regions to afford. The **controversies** surrounding the GM revolution go beyond human health to environmental issues, as well. There is fear that pest-resistant genes could spread beyond farm fields, introducing toxins to the food supplies of insects and other organisms.

For the time being, concerns over GMOs have led many governments, particularly in Europe, to strictly regulate the use and labeling of these organisms, banning them outright in some cases. Ultimately, though, the choice lies with the individual consumer. Given the potential benefits and risks, what decision would you make?

On Your Own

Have you or someone you know ever had an allergic reaction to a certain substance?

cold spell a period of lower than normal temperatures
drought a period with an extreme shortage of rainfall
produce food grown in large quantities to be sold
pharmaceutical related to the production of medicines
controversy a dispute with intense reactions on both sides

Vocabulary Building

[1-6] Complete each sentence with one of the words from the box.

advantage / shortcut / regulate / ultimately / contamination / adverse

1. Taking a(n) ______________ may save time, but often leads to problems.

2. The ______________ from the factory made the town's water undrinkable.

3. The boxer's long arms give him a(n) ______________ over his opponents.

4. Plastic products can have a(n) ______________ effect on the environment.

5. The government needs to ______________ companies in order to protect consumers.

6. Steve changed his mind several times, but ______________ decided to quit his job.

[7-12] Choose the words that are closest in meaning to the underlined ones.

7. Some spiders can <u>alter</u> the color of their skin to blend into their surrounding.
a. repair b. lend c. trust d. change

8. <u>Proponents</u> of animal rights are strongly against animal testing for any reason.
a. opponents b. advocates c. messengers d. witnesses

9. After you <u>insert</u> a coin into the machine, the game will start.
a. install b. lose c. put d. remove

10. We decided to <u>transfer</u> several employees to a new office.
a. hold b. relocate c. exchange d. alienate

11. A microphone was <u>implanted</u> deep within the secret agent's ear.
a. loosened b. felt c. connected d. embedded

12. People who are comfortable with gadgets are more likely to <u>embrace</u> new technology.
a. judge b. ignore c. imitate d. welcome

[13-15] Complete each sentence with the following idioms.

for the time being / in place of / bring about

13. To make the dish spicier, use hot peppers ___________________ tomatoes.

14. The principal's new policies ___________________ many positive changes at the school.

15. One day I'd like to get a place of my own, but I'm living with my parents _______________.

Reading Comprehension

1 What is the passage mainly about?

a. both sides of the controversy regarding GM foods
b. concerns over the use of genetically modified organisms
c. the history of the ban on GM foods in Europe
d. forms of genetic engineering used in agriculture

2 What did scientists realize about the genes used in GM foods?

a. They often produced unexpected characteristics in GMOs.
b. They required more time to mature than selectively bred genes.
c. They were more useful for the pharmaceutical industry than for agriculture.
d. They could be derived from non-plant sources.

3 Why are GM foods criticized as a solution to world hunger?

a. They aren't nutritious enough.
b. They are too expensive for poor farmers.
c. They don't require pesticides.
d. They may create stronger crops.

4 The word alleging in the passage is closest in meaning to

a. claiming
b. rejecting
c. researching
d. discouraging

5 Which of the following is NOT mentioned as an advantage of GM foods?

a. They are cheaper to manufacture.
b. They result in higher crop yields.
c. They require fewer pesticide treatments.
d. They can be supplemented with vitamins.

6 What can be inferred about the centuries-old practice of selective breeding?

a. It originated in North America.
b. It is a form of genetic modification.
c. It is not effective for controlling crop characteristics.
d. It is not a widely used technique.

7 How did scientists create the first GMOs in the 1980s?

8 What are the most common GM crops?

9 What environmental threat do GM foods pose?

Summary

Step 1 **Read the passage again and complete the outline with the words below.**

selective / deliver / inserting / resistant / beginning / allergies / harmful
faster / health / advantages / reduce / characteristics / drawbacks

I. Genetically modified foods: an old concept

A. Started with ____________ breeding: selecting certain ____________

II. The ____________ of genetically modified foods

A. ____________ and easier to control than selective breeding

B. ____________ genetic material from other sources into crops

III. ____________ of GM crops

A. ____________ to bad growing conditions

B. ____________ the need for pesticides

C. ____________ nutrients and pharmaceuticals to the developing world

IV. ____________ of GM crops

A. Potential for unforeseen long-term ____________ effects

B. Cause adverse reactions in some people with ____________

C. Patent-protected, unaffordable to poor farmers

D. Possibly environmentally ____________

Step 2 **Complete the summary with your own words based on the outline.**

Genetic modification of food is an old concept, going back to the practice of ________ breeding, which enabled farmers to select certain ____________ in their crops. ____
____
____
____
____________________ Additionally, they are patent-protected and unaffordable to poor farmers, and they are possibly environmentally ____________.

Unit 10: The History of Salt

Getting Started

1. Look at the picture. What do you think it is?
2. What are some uses for salt?
3. What kinds of salt do you know?

Building Background Knowledge

Salt information

Throughout human history, salt has filled two important roles. The first is biological, as it is a compound that many forms of animal life, including humans, cannot live without. Within our bodies, salt regulates water content, keeping our internal fluids in balance. A diet lacking in salt can cause muscle cramps, dizziness, and neurological problems. In the severest cases, prolonged lack of salt may eventually result in death. Secondly, salt is an excellent preservative, used to dry food and prevent contamination by mold, fungi, and bacteria. Historically, salt was essential for food storage, as people needed a way to ensure that stores of their harvests could sustain them during the winter, or in times of drought. Today, salt is already added to most food we purchase, and refrigeration provides a more convenient preservation method.

▲ Salt from the ocean

UNIT 10

The History of Salt

The Big Question

How has salt influenced human history?

▸ Notes

There is perhaps no single substance so vital to life yet so often taken for granted in modern times as salt. Throughout history, salt has played pivotal roles in human health as an **agent** of both nutrition and food **preservation**. Salt is so important, in fact, that in the past access to it could determine the success or failure of a population.

Humans have collected naturally occurring salt for **millennia**. Such natural sources are found in rocky pools near coastlines, where seawater is trapped and **evaporates**, leaving behind its salt content. Further inland there are salt springs, mineral-rich water that can be heated using sunlight or fire to remove its salt. Additionally, some mountainous areas, such as those of Western and Central Europe, contain salt-bearing rocks. Many of the earliest cities were founded and thrived specifically due to their **proximity** to a natural salt source.

The ancient world was made up of regions where salt was abundant and others where it was not; therefore, salt was one of the original **motivators** for trade. Given the weight of the commodity, it was most easily transported by boat. Evidence has been uncovered of a Mayan salt production center in Guatemala located next to a principal **riverine** trading route. The marine salt trade in the Mediterranean region, from ancient Roman to medieval times, is well documented, and Marco Polo noted during his visit to China that salt was shipped from the coast up the Yangtze River in great quantities.

The high value of salt provided great power to those who controlled

agent something used to achieve a particular purpose
preservation the process of keeping something from decaying
millennia thousands of years
evaporate to change into vapor
proximity the state of being near something

► Notes

its distribution, and many of history's great cities owed their **affluence** to it. Venice, for example, gained prominence partly as a result of the salt gathered in its lagoons. By the 10th century A.D., Venice had become one of the Mediterranean's most prolific salt producers and a strong Italian city-state, and it set out to dominate the salt market. Salt-making centers run by its rivals were destroyed, and wars were waged with other city-states over control of the salt trade. By 1350, Venice had secured a **monopoly**, and all salt produced in the Adriatic region had to pass through Venice, where its price was marked up substantially before it could be sold. The wealth derived from this trade helped **fuel** the artistic and scientific innovations of the Italian Renaissance.

▲ Taqcha Khana salt mine in Namak Aab district of Takhar province, northeast of Kabul

The role salt has played throughout history, in Venice and beyond, is impressive. Columbus' voyage of discovery to the New World was financed by salt production in Southern Spain. France's territorial expansions under Napoleon were largely paid for by a tax charged on salt purchases, and the State of New York used a similar tax to fund the creation of its 363-mile Erie Canal. Consider this history the next time you pick up a shaker to sprinkle salt on your meal.

On Your Own

Do you enjoy eating salty foods? Why or why not?

motivator something that makes you want to do something
riverine relating to a river
affluence a large amount of money or valuable goods
monopoly exclusive control of an industry or market by only one person or group
fuel to increase in intensity

Vocabulary Building

[1-6] Complete each sentence with one of the words from the box.

throughout / remove / note / secure / waged / prominence

1. A great battle was ____________ between the Greeks and the Persians.
2. When you enter the classroom, please ____________ how well-behaved the students are.
3. He rose to ____________ in the music industry after the release of his second album.
4. I will be checking up on your progress ____________ the day.
5. After several phone calls, I was able to ____________ tickets to the show.
6. The firemen tried to ____________ the child from the collapsed house.

[7-12] Choose the words that are closest in meaning to the underlined ones.

7. One <u>pivotal</u> battle can change the course of an entire war.
   a. final b. lengthy c. crucial d. trivial
8. Food is <u>abundant</u> in regions where the soil has many nutrients.
   a. scarce b. useful c. plentiful d. fragile
9. Once nearly extinct, bald eagles now <u>thrive</u> in many parts of North America.
   a. flourish b. suffer c. congregate d. remain
10. Our company's great products are sure to <u>dominate</u> the electronics industry.
    a. house b. lose c. remake d. control
11. Farming is the <u>principal</u> source of income for communities in the old village.
    a. main b. minor c. mistaken d. conventional
12. He was not particularly <u>prolific</u>, creating only one or two paintings a year.
    a. famous b. understood c. productive d. practical

[13-15] Complete each sentence with the following idioms.

pick up / set out to / take for granted

13. I want you to ____________ every dirty item of clothing on your bedroom floor.
14. Electronic wonders are ____________ by many young people.
15. We didn't ____________ invent a new method; it just happened by accident.

Reading Comprehension

1 What is the passage mainly about?

a. why naturally occurring salt is so valuable today
b. how our need for salt has decreased over time
c. salt's impact on civilizations throughout history
d. the uses of salt other than for preservation

2 What did the Chinese have in common with the ancient Mayans?

a. They utilized river routes to ship salt.
b. They produced salt in coastal areas.
c. They became powerful with salt money.
d. They invited foreigners to inspect their salt trade.

3 Which of the following was the salt trade responsible for funding?

a. New York's construction of a large dam
b. land gains by the French Empire
c. voyages of discovery throughout southern Spain
d. improvements in infrastructure in Venice

4 The word commodity in the passage is closest in meaning to

a. agenda
b. vessel
c. product
d. currency

5 Which of the following is NOT mentioned as a natural source of salt?

a. mineral-rich spring water
b. ancient evaporated oceans
c. salt rocks in and around mountains
d. shallow coastal lagoons

6 What can be inferred about the salt sold under Venice's monopoly?

a. It was much more expensive than salt had been in the past.
b. It was distributed far beyond the Adriatic region.
c. It was of a poorer quality than salt sold in previous eras.
d. It was produced primarily in the lagoons near Venice.

7 How did salt promote trade?

8 What two features made salt so valuable in the past?

9 What did Venice have to do in order to take over the salt trade?

Summary

Step 1 **Read the passage again and complete the outline with the words below.**

natural / cities / evidence / power / impact / monopoly
mountains / trade / importance / Venice / commodities

I. Historical ____________ of salt

A. Determined success or failure of populations

II. Salt collected from ____________ sources

A. Coastlines, springs, and ____________ contain natural salt

B. Early ____________ were built to be close to salt sources

III. Salt motivated ____________

A. Salt was one of the primary early ____________

B. ____________ of salt trade exists for many historical civilizations

IV. Control of salt led to ____________

A. ____________ produced salt and fought to dominate the market

B. Money from Venice's salt ____________ helped start the Renaissance

V. Salt's great ____________ on history

A. Many important historical events were made possible by salt

Step 2 **Complete the summary with your own words based on the outline.**

Salt has been very ____________ throughout history, even determining the success or failure of populations. ____

____

____

____

____

____ Salt has had a great ____________ on history, and many important events were made possible by salt.

Unit 11: The Cultural Advances of Hellenism

Getting Started

1. Look at the two pictures. Can you find some differences between them?
2. What do you know about ancient Greece?
3. Imagine that you are the ruler of many countries. Would you prefer to combine the various cultures or keep them separate?

Building Background Knowledge

Alexander the Great (356-323 B.C.)

Alexander the Great was born to Philip II of Macedon and his wife, Olympias, in 356 B.C. He received a classical Greek education under the philosopher Aristotle and military training in the Macedonian army. In 336 B.C., Alexander took over the throne, inheriting both a large kingdom and a strong military.

The young king began his rule with plans of expansion that had been drawn up by his father. He first led his army through Asia Minor before moving on to Syria, Egypt, Mesopotamia, Persia, and Bactria. By 331 B.C., he had conquered the entire Persian Empire without having lost a single battle.

Alexander spread the Greek language and culture throughout each of the territories he acquired and succeeded in uniting his empire by allowing Macedonians, Greeks, and Persians to work side-by-side in positions of government. Aiming to fuse the various civilizations, he married two Persian noblewomen and required his generals to do the same. Thus, a new culture combining ideas from the Mediterranean and Asia spread throughout a large part of the known world.

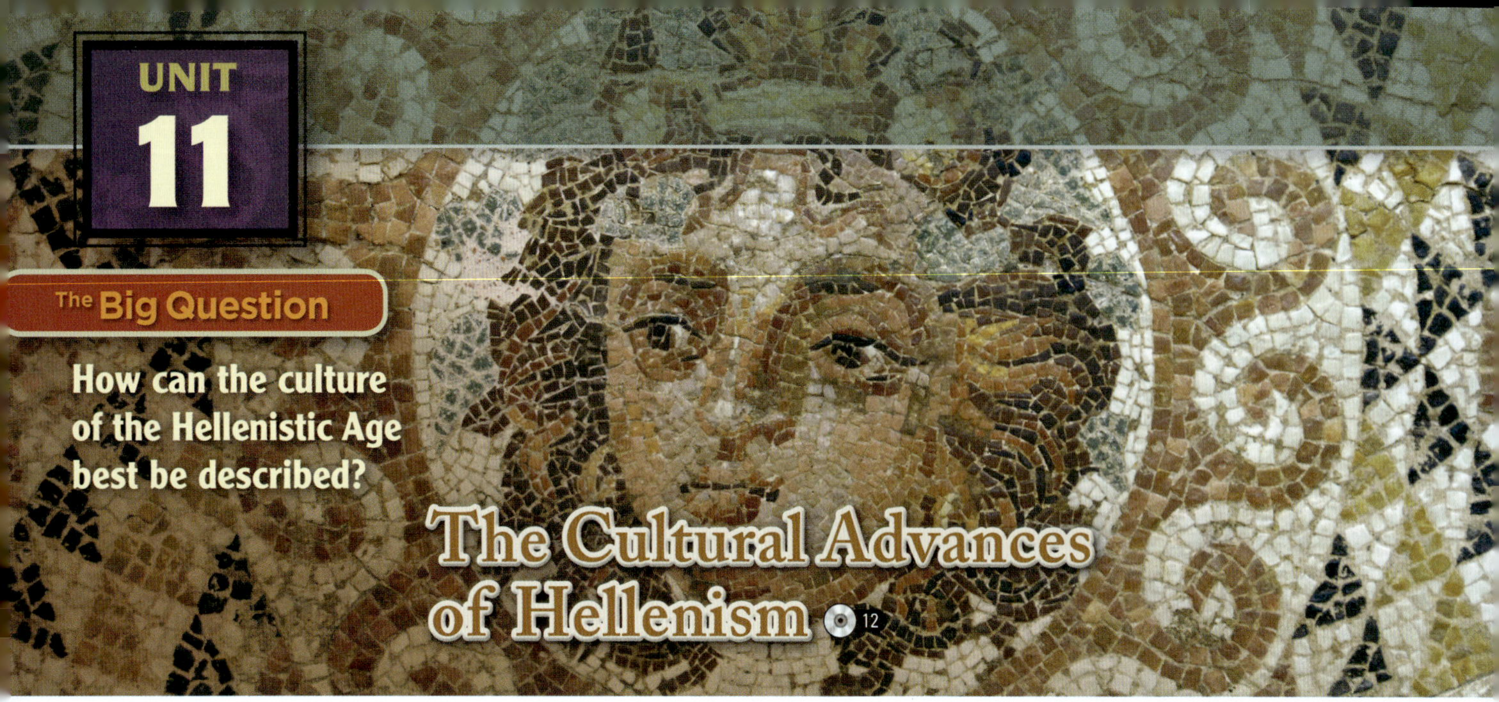

UNIT 11

The Big Question

How can the culture of the Hellenistic Age best be described?

The Cultural Advances of Hellenism

▸ Notes

The Hellenistic Age refers to an **epoch** when Greek culture held sway from the Mediterranean to parts of modern-day India. This **dominance** was the immediate result of the military **prowess** of Alexander the Great, a Greek-educated Macedonian who, in little more than a decade, built the ancient world's largest empire. Alexander promoted the diffusion of Greek culture by encouraging interracial marriages and inviting Greek merchants and scholars to settle throughout his empire. Even after his sudden death in 323 B.C., Greek influence continued to radiate, intermingling with local customs and institutions.

Alexander's empire was **subsequently** divided by his generals into a number of smaller kingdoms. Though separate politically, each **hosted** the distinct Hellenistic culture that had emerged. In some regards, Hellenism resembled Classical Greek culture—the Greek language was employed by rulers and the upper classes, for example—but many other elements of Classicism, including democratic rule, were abandoned. The Hellenistic Age also witnessed the rise of commercial hubs that profited from new opportunities in international trade. Cities like Alexandria, Egypt and Antioch, Syria were transformed by this explosion in commerce. Their newfound wealth attracted thousands of immigrants from all over Greece, who further contributed to the vibrant culture that had developed.

As in Classical Greece, philosophers were active under Hellenism, only now, instead of **pondering** the universe's ultimate truths, they advocated **ethical** conduct and human happiness. Several schools of thought formed

epoch a specific period in history
dominance the condition of being powerful
prowess exceptional ability or skill
subsequently happening after
host to provide a place for

► Notes

with this aim. The Stoics believed humans should divorce themselves from emotion and concern for material well-being to achieve happiness. The Skeptics preached the virtue of doubt, while the Cynics called for a return to a more primitive manner of existence.

Elaborating on a broad base of Greek and non-Greek traditions, Hellenistic scientists made many **advances**, with the astronomer Aristarchus becoming one of the earliest to argue that Earth circled the sun. Also, **disciplines** that to this day define the study of mathematics—trigonometry, geometry, and calculus—had their foundations laid by the Hellenistic figures Hipparchus, Euclid, and Archimedes, respectively.

▲ *Venus de Milo*

Developments in philosophy and science were matched by those in literature and the arts. A simplified form of the Greek language called Koine was formulated, making texts more accessible to audiences in Hellenistic lands, and important literary works, such as the Jewish Old Testament, were translated into Greek. Significant changes in sculpture occurred during this time as well. Whereas Classical sculptors had focused solely on idealized human forms, usually those of young males, they now began depicting children, women, and the elderly, all in striking naturalistic detail. The world-renowned *Venus de Milo* dates from this period.

Despite their cultural achievements, the Hellenistic dynasties were unable to maintain political stability. Many small independent kingdoms gradually broke away, and by 200 B.C., a new regional power was on the rise: Imperial Rome. Between 146 and 31 B.C., Rome conquered the last **vestiges** of Alexander the Great's once mighty empire, yet these successors adopted much more of Hellenistic culture than they destroyed. The philosophical, scientific, and artistic progress achieved under Hellenism survived to influence countless civilizations, including many aspects of our modern world.

On Your Own

Which culture has had the most profound impact on the place where you live?

ponder to think deeply about something
ethical conforming to the standards of what is deemed right
advance progress in development
discipline an area of knowledge that people study
vestige a remainder of something that once existed

Vocabulary Building

[1-6] Complete each sentence with one of the words from the box.

advocate / abandon / emerge / accessible / elaborate / whereas

1. Sally became a lawyer to ____________ for the rights of mistreated people.

2. We saw a family of deer ____________ from the forest shortly after the sun set.

3. Reading aids make our books ____________ to people with visual disabilities.

4. He didn't ____________ his dream of becoming a doctor even during the hardest times.

5. At that time, Europe was still divided into small kingdoms, ____________ China had already unified.

6. The boss asked him to ____________ on the more complicated parts of his plan.

[7-12] Choose the words that are closest in meaning to the underlined ones.

7. A mistranslation led Michelangelo to <u>depict</u> Moses with horns on his forehead.
a. represent b. pose c. finalize d. support

8. The Litchfield Women's Club received a gold plaque for its <u>significant</u> donation.
a. major b. kind c. surprising d. extra

9. Petroleum corporations and construction firms are <u>profiting</u> most from the war.
a. charging b. expecting c. earning d. growing

10. It costs the state more than a billion dollars a year to <u>maintain</u> its roads.
a. prepare b. secure c. map d. keep up

11. Many public schools want to <u>adopt</u> school uniforms to reduce peer pressure.
a. distrust b. use c. regulate d. emphasize

12. It took Dr. Katz many years of hard work to <u>formulate</u> the measles vaccine.
a. devise b. explain c. study d. promote

[13-15] Complete each sentence with the following idioms.

call for / divorce from / hold sway

13. Protestors are ______________ a ban on junk food advertising.

14. The investors' needs are sure to ______________ over the company's future direction.

15. Anti-materialists say that we cannot be happy until we ______________ ourselves ______________ our possessions.

Reading Comprehension

1 What is the main idea of the passage?

a. The Hellenistic Age encouraged increased creativity in literature and the arts.
b. Roman culture had more of a lasting impact on the world than Greek culture did.
c. Hellenism expanded on Greek culture to realize innovations in many fields.
d. Alexander founded an empire with the specific goal of spreading Greek influence.

2 What became of Hellenism after the fall of the Hellenistic dynasties?

a. It was replaced by the culture of Imperial Rome.
b. It was adopted by the Romans and passed to other civilizations.
c. It was maintained only in small, independent kingdoms.
d. It was rediscovered by thinkers in the modern world.

3 Why did foreign cities like Alexandria become important centers of Hellenistic culture?

a. They were places located close to mainland Greece.
b. They adopted democracy and other aspects of Greek society.
c. They were based around large Greek military encampments.
d. They became centers of trade with large Greek populations.

4 The word vibrant in the passage is closest in meaning to

a. bright b. dynamic
c. attractive d. separate

5 Which of the following is NOT an example of a difference between Hellenism and Classicism?

a. the primary focus of philosophers
b. the main method of governance
c. the subject matter used by sculptors
d. the language used by the elite

6 What can be inferred about Greek literature prior to the introduction of Koine?

a. It dealt mostly with absolute truths of the universe.
b. Many Hellenistic citizens were unable to read it.
c. There were no religious texts written in Greek.
d. Books were widespread in the Hellenistic kingdoms.

7 How did Alexander the Great enable the spread of Greek culture?

8 How did Hellenistic sculpture differ from Classical sculpture?

9 How did Hellenistic thinkers contribute to the study of mathematics?

Summary

Step 1 **Read the passage again and complete the outline with the words below.**

cultural / mathematicians / literature / birth / Rome / philosophers
happiness / Romans / Hellenism / realistic / Greek / survival

I. The ______________ of Hellenism

A. Alexander the Great founded a vast empire and encouraged the spread of ______________ culture

B. Greek culture mixed with local customs to create ______________

II. Hellenistic ______________ achievements

A. ______________ formulated different methods for achieving ______________

B. Scientists and ______________ produced new theories and disciplines

C. ______________ was expanded through a simplified version of Greek

D. Sculptors took up a more ______________ style

III. The ______________ of Hellenism

A. Hellenistic kingdoms lost control and were conquered by ______________

B. The ______________ adopted much of Hellenism and spread it to other peoples

Step 2 **Complete the summary with your own words based on the outline.**

Alexander the Great's military conquests saw the expansion of ______________ influence over a vast empire. ____

____

____

____

____

____

____ However, __________ adopted many principles of Hellenism and furthered their spread among the peoples of the region.

Unit 12: Impressionism

Getting Started

1 Look at the painting. What features make the painting special?

2 Do you know what "impressionism" means? Can you guess what kind of art movement it was?

3 Have you heard of Edgar Degas, Claude Monet, or Pierre-Auguste Renoir? If you have, do you know any of their works?

Building Background Knowledge

The Rise of the Impressionism

There were two major factors behind the rise of the Impressionist movement. The first was the growing popularity of photography. As cameras grew smaller and became more affordable, candid photographs began to replace formal studio compositions. These pictures inspired the Impressionists to use their own medium to capture people in natural settings and everyday situations as well. Furthermore, Impressionists sought to separate their paintings from photographs by adding a subjective interpretation to their depictions, something photographers could not do. The second major influence behind Impressionism was the arrival of Japanese art prints in Europe. Originally brought into France as wrapping paper for other Japanese goods, they had a profound effect on a number of the Impressionists. Many of the unconventional angles and perspectives in Impressionist art can be traced directly to these prints.

▲ A young girl posing in a studio

▲ Candid photograph of a young girl in a zoo

UNIT 12

The Big Question

What is Impressionism?

Impressionism

13

▸ Notes

The Impressionist **movement** began in the late 1860s in France and was led by artists such as Edgar Degas, Edouard Manet, Claude Monet, and Pierre-Auguste Renoir. Impressionism was a new style of painting that aimed to capture the artist's sensory **impressions** of a subject rather than to reproduce reality. It was a revolt against the strict rules of traditional academic painting whose standards were set by France's Academie des Beaux-Arts. Preferring dark colors, portraits, and historical subjects, the Academie frequently rejected the Impressionists' bright, loosely composed landscapes in its annual art show, the Salon de Paris. In an independent showing, Monet's *Impression: Sunrise* (1872), eventually won public acceptance and gave the movement its name.

▲ *Impression: Sunrise* (1872)

Impressionism was characterized by quick, expressive **brushstrokes** and the absence of sharp, defined lines. Impressionist paintings often had an "unfinished look," which was meant to portray a **fleeting**, spontaneous moment. When it came to color, Impressionist painters stayed away from the dark tones of academic paintings, and pure Impressionists avoided using black altogether. They applied bright colors next to one another on the canvas while the paints were still wet in order to create soft edges. The blending or mixing of colors was avoided. The Impressionists came to

movement a group of people who work together to obtain a certain objective
impression an image in the mind inspired by some stimulus
brushstroke the mark left by a brush
fleeting disappearing quickly
optical related to vision and the eyes

understand the **optical** effects of layering colors, which seemed to make their paintings glow with light.

▸ Notes

With the introduction of pre-mixed paints in lead tubes, Impressionist painters no longer had to grind and mix dry **pigment** powders with linseed oil in advance. As a result, they were able to work impulsively and wherever they wished. Instead of painting important people in a studio or using the canvas to tell a religious or moral story, the artists stepped outside to capture vivid scenes of nature. For this reason, they were said to be working "en plein air," which is French for "in the open air." Therefore, common themes in Impressionist paintings were scenes from everyday life, landscapes, and the modern, bustling city of Paris.

Owing to the fact that the Impressionists' works were unwelcomed by the Academie des Beaux-Arts, they set up their own independent **exhibitions**. The exhibitions were held from 1874 to 1886 and included paintings by Paul Cezanne, Berthe Morisot, Camille Pissarro, Renoir, Monet, and Degas. A majority of art critics had found the Impressionist paintings formless, incomplete, and unsophisticated; however, they were rather successful with the general public. So, while it was not understood or appreciated by everyone, the Impressionist movement flourished for about two decades.

Impressionism had a profound impact on other French painters as well as on artists around the world. The artists who followed developed new techniques and movements like **Pointillism**, Post-Impressionism, **Cubism**, **Expressionism** and Modernism based on the developments made by Impressionists. Impressionism also spread to other areas, with French composer Claude Debussy leading the movement in music. Musical Impressionism turned away from the formal pieces of composers such as Wolfgang Amadeus Mozart and Ludwig van Beethoven and focused on tonal color and mood. The Impressionists' legacy, then, is perhaps that they paved the way for artists of all mediums to experiment with their techniques and materials.

On Your Own

What kind of artwork do you have in your house? Describe it.

pigment a substance that contributes color
exhibition a display of art
Pointillism a style of painting that produces images with many small dots of color
Cubism 20th century style of painting that was geometrical and abstract
Expressionism colorful and symbolic style of painting representing the artist's inner experience

Vocabulary Building

[1-6] Complete each sentence with one of the words from the box.

apply / impulsively / expressive / critic / scenes / bustling

1. At that age, children sometimes act ___________, doing what they want, when they want.

2. The opera singer's ___________ voice makes the character's pain so real for me.

3. We'll have to ___________ another layer of paint to the wall so it doesn't look so spotty.

4. It is always hard to find a seat in the ___________ café.

5. This photographer hikes a lot and typically takes pictures of mountain ___________.

6. He has a reputation as the harshest food ___________ in the restaurant business.

[7-12] Choose the words that are closest in meaning to the underlined ones.

7. The 1960s television series *Star Trek* had a profound cultural impact.

a. costly　b. accepted　c. famous　d. deep

8. It takes great artistic skill to portray a facial expression as fascinating as Mona Lisa's.

a. interpret　b. represent　c. conceive of　d. compare with

9. He's too unsophisticated to tell the difference between an expensive piece of chocolate and a cheap one.

a. appropriate　b. simple　c. predictable　d. unhealthy

10. The teacher told students to forget the rules of formal poetry and write freely.

a. truthful　b. brief　c. popular　d. structured

11. When young artists started moving in, the neighborhood began to flourish again.

a. demolish　b. intercept　c. expand　d. thrive

12. Many failed to appreciate Chopin in his day because his work was ahead of its time.

a. value　b. ignore　c. challenge　d. retreat

[13-15] Complete each sentence with the following idioms.

owing to / mean to / in advance

13. If you'd like to reserve a copy of the book, you'll have to pay ___________.

14. I ___________ turn in my assignment today, but I left it at home.

15. ___________ the bad weather, the picnic was rescheduled for next week.

Reading Comprehension

1 What is the main idea of the passage?

a. The Academie des Beaux-Arts restricted many artists.
b. An innovative style of painting redefined the arts in France.
c. Pre-mixed paints revolutionized the standards of European art.
d. French artists impacted the everyday lives of the people.

2 What legacy did the Impressionists leave behind?

a. They made experimentation of art forms possible.
b. They improved the standards of academic painting.
c. They invalidated the Academie des Beaux-Arts.
d. They altered the tone and mood of classical music.

3 Where did Impressionism get its name?

a. It was based on the reaction of the general public.
b. It was created by the Academie des Beaux-Arts.
c. It came from the title of an Impressionist painting.
d. A group of Impressionist artists invented the term.

4 The word spontaneous in the passage is closest in meaning to

a. spiritual b. uncontrolled
c. organized d. deliberate

5 Which of the following is NOT a characteristic of Impressionism?

a. bright tones
b. unfinished edges
c. blended colors
d. layered paint

6 What can be inferred about musical Impressionists?

a. They composed music to tell a dramatic story.
b. They preferred long forms of music like the symphony.
c. They aimed to create a certain mood or atmosphere.
d. They used standard harmonic progressions.

7 Which aspects of academic painting did Impressionist painters rebel against?

8 How did pre-mixed paints affect Impressionism?

9 What impact did Impressionism have on art around the world?

Summary

Step 1 **Read the passage again and complete the outline with the words below.**

Impressionist / academic / blending / open air / brushstrokes
France / musical / techniques / impulsively / appreciated / legacy / rejected

I. The ____________ movement

A. Began in the late 1860s in ____________

B. Revolt against strict rules of ____________ painting

II. Characteristics and ____________

A. Expressive ____________, bright colors

B. Soft edges, no ____________ of colors

III. Themes

A. Painted ____________ in ____________ **B.** Everyday life, landscapes, Paris

IV. Public Reaction

A. ____________ by art critics and the Academie des Beaux-Arts

B. ____________ more or less by general public

V. Impact and ____________

A. Influenced fellow French painters and other artists around the world

B. Led to ____________ Impressionism

Step 2 **Complete the summary with your own words based on the outline.**

The ______________ movement began in the late 1860s in ____________. ________

____

____

____

____

______________________________________ It influenced other French painters and artists around the world and led to the ____________ Impressionism movement.

Unit 13: The Great Barrier Reef

Getting Started

1. Look at the picture. Describe what you see.
2. Where can you find examples of biodiversity on the planet?
3. Are there any World Heritage Sites in your country? If so, can you name them?

Building Background Knowledge

A Variety of Coral Reefs

Beautiful coral reef formations, often enormous in size, fill the warm, shallow waters of Earth's tropical oceans. There are three general types of coral reefs, categorized by the characteristics of their structure and environment. Reefs that form very near an island or some other landmass, following the outline of its coast, are known as fringing reefs. Similar in form but separated from the shore by a greater distance, barrier reefs make up the second category of coral reefs. Barrier reefs follow the contours of the coast, creating a calm, often deep lagoon between the shoreline and the open ocean. The third and final category of coral reefs is the atoll. An atoll is a reef that encloses a lagoon, like a barrier reef, the difference being that an atoll has no central island.

▲ Fringing reef

▲ Round atoll

UNIT 13

The Big Question

What are some of the current threats facing the Great Barrier Reef?

The Great Barrier Reef

14

► Notes

Off the northeast coast of Australia stretches the largest organic structure in the world, the Great Barrier Reef. It is an immense system of coral reefs that covers an area of 344,400 square kilometers in size and is visible from space.

Once thought to be plants, corals are actually composed of colonies of tiny **cylindrical** animals called polyps. When polyps feed, they **ingest** minerals like calcium, and this calcium is secreted by the polyps to form a hard skeleton around their soft bodies. Over time, as the colony expands, the skeleton grows and eventually takes on the characteristic reef structure. Coral polyps also maintain a symbiotic relationship with species of **algae**, which live inside them. Symbiotic relationships are mutually beneficial: the polyps provide the algae with a protective environment, while the algae, through **photosynthesis**, supply the polyps with food energy and are also responsible for some of the bright coloring seen in corals. Because algae require abundant sunlight to perform photosynthesis, coral reefs are found in shallow, transparent waters with warm temperatures, such as those off of Australia's Queensland coast.

The Great Barrier Reef is itself alive, but it also **harbors** extraordinary biodiversity. Due to waste **excreted** by the corals, the water around the reef is particularly nutrient rich. This attracts bacteria, plants, and **microorganisms**, which in turn encourage the presence of larger species, and so on up to the highest tier of predators like sharks and rays. It is estimated that around 1,500 species of fish and 4,000 species of **mollusks**

cylindrical shaped like a cylinder
ingest to take something into one's body
algae a simple form of plant life that lives in water
photosynthesis a process used by plants to create its own food
harbor to provide a place or habitat for something

▸ Notes

live in the Great Barrier Reef, a fact that contributed to its **designation** as a World Heritage Site in 1981.

▲ the Great Barrier Reef

Unfortunately, the world's largest coral reef system is very much in need of the protection awarded such sites. One of the most serious threats to its continued existence is human activity. Oil drilling, fishing, and tourism operations can catastrophically harm the reef, and trends like increased coastal development and the **runoff** of untreated sewage and contaminated rainwater also pose serious risks. To mitigate these factors, the Australian government created the Great Barrier Reef Marine Park in 1975. The park divides the reef into different zones, each of which carries strict guidelines on what activities are and are not permitted, and there are some areas where human activity is not allowed at all.

Another serious threat, and one that cannot be so easily controlled, comes from global warming. The algae within corals are sensitive to temperature changes in the water; a rise of just two degrees Celsius can cause them to die off. This is known as "coral bleaching," for without algae the coral loses its color and turns grayish white. While the corals can survive for a time without the algae, a prolonged absence will lead to the death of the reef. Therefore, the Great Barrier Reef serves as a kind of early warning system for the effects of global warming, demonstrating how serious the problem will become if no action is taken to curb it.

On Your Own

What can you do to help protect important environmental sites in your country?

excrete to naturally remove something from one's body
microorganism a tiny living creature
mollusk a type of sea or land animal that has a soft body usually covered by a hard shell
designation the official categorization of something
runoff excess liquid exceeding storage capacity

Vocabulary Building

[1-6] Complete each sentence with one of the words from the box.

transparent / attract / presence / strict / contaminate / permit

1. The children always grew quiet in the __________ of their stern grandfather.

2. These are __________ orders, so follow them word for word.

3. The chef sliced the potato so thin that the pieces were nearly __________.

4. If you turn on the outdoor light, it will __________ too many insects.

5. When I was a child, my parents did not __________ me to watch TV.

6. The new factory is likely to __________ several nearby lakes.

[7-12] Choose the words that are closest in meaning to the underlined ones.

7. According to the contract, our companies are <u>mutually</u> responsible for any errors.

a. frankly b. happily c. separately d. jointly

8. In order to <u>mitigate</u> the effects of the layoffs, the company offered financial counseling.

a. improve b. lessen c. finalize d. remove

9. Using the new fertilizer, the farmers grew pumpkins of <u>extraordinary</u> size.

a. youthful b. exceptional c. unremarkable d. humble

10. A briefcase held over one's head can <u>serve</u> as an umbrella in an emergency.

a. act b. represent c. hide d. receive

11. This new legislation is designed to <u>curb</u> harmful lending practices of banks.

a. abolish b. record c. encourage d. restrict

12. Watching television for <u>prolonged</u> periods could have a bad effect on your eyes.

a. abbreviated b. usual c. extended d. temporary

[13-15] Complete each sentence with the following idioms.

in turn / die off / lead to

13. If you pay for the damages, the company, __________, will withdraw their lawsuit.

14. The acid rain caused the plants growing in the area to __________.

15. His bad attitude could __________ worse behavior in the future.

Reading Comprehension

1 What is the passage mainly about?

a. the Great Barrier Reef and current threats to its existence
b. the effect of global warming on the Great Barrier Reef
c. the importance of World Heritage Sites and protected parks
d. the history of the Great Barrier Reef Marine Park

2 What factor contributed to the Great Barrier Reef's designation as a World Heritage Site?

a. its enormous size, which covers 344,400 square kilometers
b. its vulnerability to certain human activities, like oil drilling
c. its susceptibility to environmental change brought on by global warming
d. its biodiversity, which includes 5,500 species of fish and shellfish

3 What happens during the process of "coral bleaching"?

a. Rising temperatures cause reef algae to die off.
b. Coral polyps secrete a hard, white calcium substance.
c. Bacteria, plants, and microorganisms colonize coral reefs.
d. Toxic runoff seeps into and contaminates shallow reef waters.

4 The word tier in the passage is closest in meaning to

a. risk b. level
c. relevance d. diversity

5 According to the passage, which of the following is NOT true about coral polyps?

a. They are small and cylindrical and live in colonies.
b. They have soft bodies surrounded by a hard calcium outer skeleton.
c. They cause most of the bright coloration characteristic of reef structures.
d. They carry on a symbiotic relationship with certain algae.

6 What can be inferred about the Great Barrier Reef's World Heritage status?

a. It provides the site with an amount of protection.
b. It is a temporary designation to help the reef recover.
c. It is more important than its status as a marine park.
d. It discourages tourism along the Queensland coast.

7 What kinds of human activities threaten the continued survival of the Great Barrier Reef?

8 How does the Great Barrier Reef Marine Park help protect the reef site?

9 What misconception was once held about corals?

Summary

Step 1 **Read the passage again and complete the outline with the words below.**

composition / algae / nutrient / threats / polyps / shallow / biodiversity
World Heritage / human activity / marine / global warming / death

I. ______________ of the Great Barrier Reef

A. Situated in ______________ waters off the northeast coast of Australia

B. Composed of coral ______________ with calcium skeletons

C. Contains ______________ in a symbiotic relationship with polyps

II. The Great Barrier Reef's ______________

A. ______________ rich waters home to an enormous variety of fish and shellfish species

B. Named a(n) ________________ Site in 1981

III. ______________ to the Great Barrier Reef

A. ________________ like oil drilling, fishing, tourism, and coastal development

B. In 1975, it became a protected ______________ park

C. Rising water temperatures caused by ______________

D. Algae death causes coral bleaching and leads to ______________ of the reef

Step 2 **Complete the summary with your own words based on the outline.**

Situated in the ___________ waters off the northeast coast of Australia, the Great Barrier Reef is composed of coral ___________, tiny animals with calcium skeletons.

____

____

____

____

____

________ Rising water temperatures caused by __________________ also threaten the reef, as algae death causes coral bleaching and leads to the ___________ of the reef.

Unit 14: The Frozen Continent

Getting Started

1. Can you describe the climate of Antarctica?
2. Can you guess what animals live in the Antarctic?
3. How might global warming affect the Antarctic?

Building Background Knowledge

Antarctic Animals

Because it experiences temperatures more extreme than anywhere else on Earth, Antarctica is an ideal region to study in order to learn how animals adapt and survive in harsh environments. Certain physical adaptations enable Antarctic animals to stay warm in the frigid climate, such as layers of fat, thick skin, round bodies, and waterproof feathers. The blood of fish and insects has the advantageous feature of not freezing in the cold. The Weddell seal, an air-breathing sea animal, has developed the ability to hold its breath for twenty minutes while hunting underwater. Behavioral adaptations also assist animals living in the far southern reaches of the planet. For example, penguin populations have learned to huddle together for warmth, with individual penguins taking turns moving from the outer, coldest parts of the crowd toward the warmer inner portion. Whales deal with the Antarctic winter by migrating, to wait out the cold in warmer waters.

▲ Mother and baby Emperor penguin with a close-up of waterproof feathers

UNIT 14

The Frozen Continent

The Big Question

In what ways is Antarctica different from other continents?

▸ Notes

Sitting directly over the South Pole and blanketed by thick ice, Antarctica is a continent of extremes. Its desert-like climate has an average year round temperature of –49 degrees Celsius, making it both the most frigid and one of the most **arid** places on Earth. Stronger winds have been recorded on Antarctica than anywhere else, and the continent's average elevation is more than three times that of any other. Surrounded by three oceans, it is as large as Mexico and the United States combined, and in the depths of winter it receives absolutely no sunlight.

Though temperatures in Antarctica are always chilling, variations exist depending on season and **region**. The lowest occur in the continent's interior, where the average remains under –30 degrees Celsius even in summer and drops to –65 degrees in winter. On the coast, conversely, summer can bring above-freezing temperatures, but these plunge to between –10 and –20 degrees Celsius in winter. Water in the surrounding seas either freezes to form loose sea ice or hovers just above freezing.

Antarctica's **inhospitable** climate makes permanent human settlement impossible, but the frozen continent provides a home for many other species, which live in the oceans around the landmass, in coastal **habitats**, or both. Within the marine ecosystem, tiny organisms called phytoplankton harness the energy of the sun through photosynthesis and are consumed by krill, small shrimp-like animals. Krill, in turn, serve as the primary food source for a number of larger species, including fish, whales, and penguin chicks. Seals and bird species make up the rest of the

arid characterized by scarcity of water
region a large area of land
inhospitable not accommodating for life
habitat the area where a plant or animal lives
inhabitant someone or something that lives in an area

Antarctic animal community.

Antarctica hosts human **inhabitants** as well, researchers engaged in projects at the continent's science stations. **Fields** as diverse as astronomy, biology, and volcanology are regularly investigated on the continent. By international **treaty**, Antarctica is regarded as a "Zone of Peace;" all countries have access to it and are free to conduct research as they see fit, provided it does not harm the environment or **infringe** on the rights of teams from other nations. The American-operated McMurdo Station is the largest human settlement on Antarctica, capable of supporting as many as 1,258 residents.

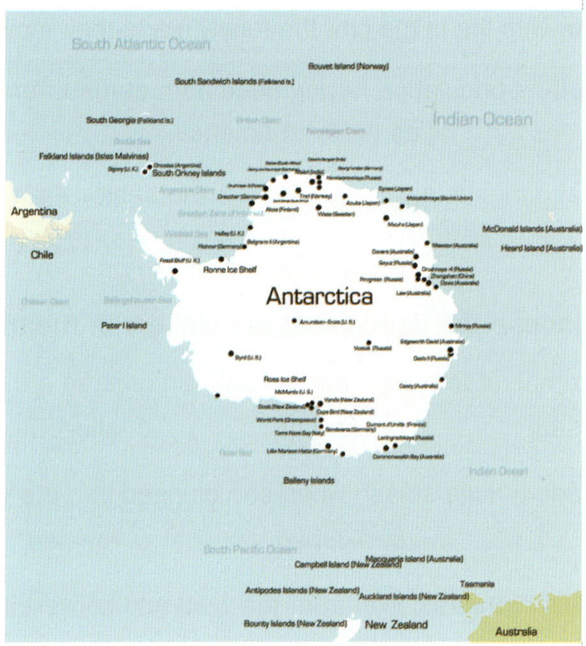

Unfortunately, though sometimes well intentioned, human activity does not always leave the Antarctic environment unscathed. Tourism is a growing concern, as more cruise ships visit the Antarctic Ocean every year and sometimes dispose of waste improperly, as do the science stations, which have even contaminated the surrounding landscape with **radioactive** waste. However, the greatest threat to Antarctica, and consequently the rest of the world, comes from global warming. Rising sea and air temperatures are weakening the Antarctic ice sheet, causing massive chunks of ice to detach and enter the open ocean. This trend has the potential to raise sea levels around the world by more than a meter, **presaging** severe flooding of coastal areas. Clearly, action should be taken to preserve Antarctica, both for the sake of the animals that call it home and the security of millions of people worldwide.

► Notes

On Your Own

What do you do to protect your local environment?

field an area of study or investigation
treaty an official document of understanding
infringe to violate something that is not one's own
radioactive having the ability to produce harmful energy
presage to warn of a future event

Vocabulary Building

[1-6] Complete each sentence with one of the words from the box.

diverse / permanent / hovered / blanket / preserve / absolutely

1. Around Christmastime, a thick layer of snow will ______________ the entire city.

2. The office was ______________ silent until someone sneezed.

3. The value of the dollar ______________ around that of the yen all year.

4. Unhappy with life in the city, the family made their move to the countryside ______________.

5. With half its population having been born abroad, Toronto is one of the most ______________ cities in North America.

6. National parks help ______________ the habitats of many endangered plants and animals.

[7-12] Choose the words that are closest in meaning to the underlined ones.

7. <u>Frigid</u> temperatures after a period of rain created a thin layer of ice on the roads.
a. unusual b. extreme c. alleged d. freezing

8. She made a huge splash when she <u>plunged</u> into the water.
a. slid b. skipped c. roamed d. dove

9. Windmills <u>harness</u> power from the wind and convert it to electricity.
a. cooperate b. determine c. distribute d. utilize

10. A manatee will typically <u>consume</u> about 100 pounds of seagrass in a single day.
a. eat b. sift c. grow d. flush

11. Children who <u>engage</u> in outdoor activities are happier than those who don't.
a. decline b. participate c. support d. lack

12. The recession progressed until the nation was in <u>severe</u> economic trouble.
a. grave b. worthwhile c. sickened d. false

[13-15] Complete each sentence with the following idioms.

a number of / make up / for the sake of

13. Consumers ought to spend more ________________ the national economy.

14. Polish Americans ________________ a relatively small portion of the U.S. population.

15. ________________ people showed interest in knitting, so they decided to form a club.

Reading Comprehension

1 What is the passage mainly about?

a. the environmental impact of human activities on Antarctica
b. the climate of, inhabitants of, and threats to Antarctica
c. the biology, ecology, and volcanology of Antarctica
d. the history of Antarctic exploration and current research projects

2 What role do phytoplankton play in Antarctica's marine ecosystem?

a. They oxygenate the frozen oceans for other organisms, like whales and seals.
b. They feed on krill and other tiny aquatic organisms.
c. They provide a food source for small species in the region.
d. They make up the most populous class of organisms in Antarctica.

3 In what way does the growing tourism industry affect Antarctica?

a. It creates international tensions due to competition in tourism.
b. It encourages and raises funds for Antarctic research.
c. It contaminates the region with waste from cruise ships.
d. It promotes environmental stewardship among travelers.

4 The word unscathed in the passage is closest in meaning to

a. safe
b. long-lasting
c. exposed
d. fragile

5 Which of the following is NOT mentioned as a current threat to Antarctica?

a. contamination from scientific research stations
b. increasing water and air temperatures
c. flooding along the continent's shorelines
d. the effects of tourism on the continent

6 What can be inferred about the international treaty?

a. It has not managed to foster international cooperation.
b. It has resulted in the development of Antarctic tourism.
c. It has failed to protect the environment from contamination.
d. It has contributed to the problem of global warming.

7 What are average temperatures like in Antarctica?

8 Why is Antarctica considered a "Zone of Peace"?

9 What makes immediate action to preserve Antarctica necessary?

Summary

Step 1 **Read the passage again and complete the outline with the words below.**

freezing / human / settlement / inhabitants / climate
global warming / driest / phytoplankton / tourism / effects / open

I. ______________ of Antarctica

A. One of the coldest and ______________ places on the planet

B. Often below ______________, even in summer

II. Non-human ______________ of Antarctica

A. ______________ makes energy from sunlight

B. Krill, fish, whales, seals, and birds also inhabit Antarctica

III. Temporary ______________ population on Antarctica

A. McMurdo Station the largest human ______________

B. As a Zone of Peace, it is ______________ to science teams from all countries

IV. ______________ of human activities on Antarctica

A. ______________ and research contaminate the environment

B. ______________ weakening Antarctic ice sheet

C. Steps necessary to protect Antarctica and people worldwide

Step 2 **Complete the summary with your own words based on the outline.**

Antarctica is one of the coldest and ________ places on the planet, with temperatures that are often below ________, even in the summer. ______________________________

____

____

____

____

____ Because of this, it is necessary to take steps to protect Antarctica and people all over the world.

Unit 15: The Birth of the Skyscraper

Getting Started

1. Can you name the tallest building in the world?
2. What is the tallest building in your country?
3. What kinds of technology do we need to build tall buildings?

Building Background Knowledge

Skyscraper Race

1 The United Arab Emirates renamed its Burj Dubai building **Burj Khalifa** in honor of the current UAE president Sheikh Khalifa bin Zayed al Nahyan when it was officially opened on January 4, 2010. It is presently the tallest building in the world.

2 Taipei, Taiwan's 101-story **Taipei Financial Center**(or Taipei 101) was the tallest building in the world from 2004 to 2010.

3 The **Petronas Twin Towers** in Kuala Lumpur, Malaysia were the world's tallest buildings from 1998 to 2004 thanks to their tall spires.

4 Located in Chicago, Illinois, the 108-story Sears Tower was the world's tallest building from 1974 to 1998. It was renamed the **Willis Tower** in 2009.

5 The **World Trade Center Twin Towers** in New York City were the tallest buildings in the world from 1972 to 1973.

6 New York City's 102-story **Empire State Building** was the world's tallest building from 1931 to 1972.

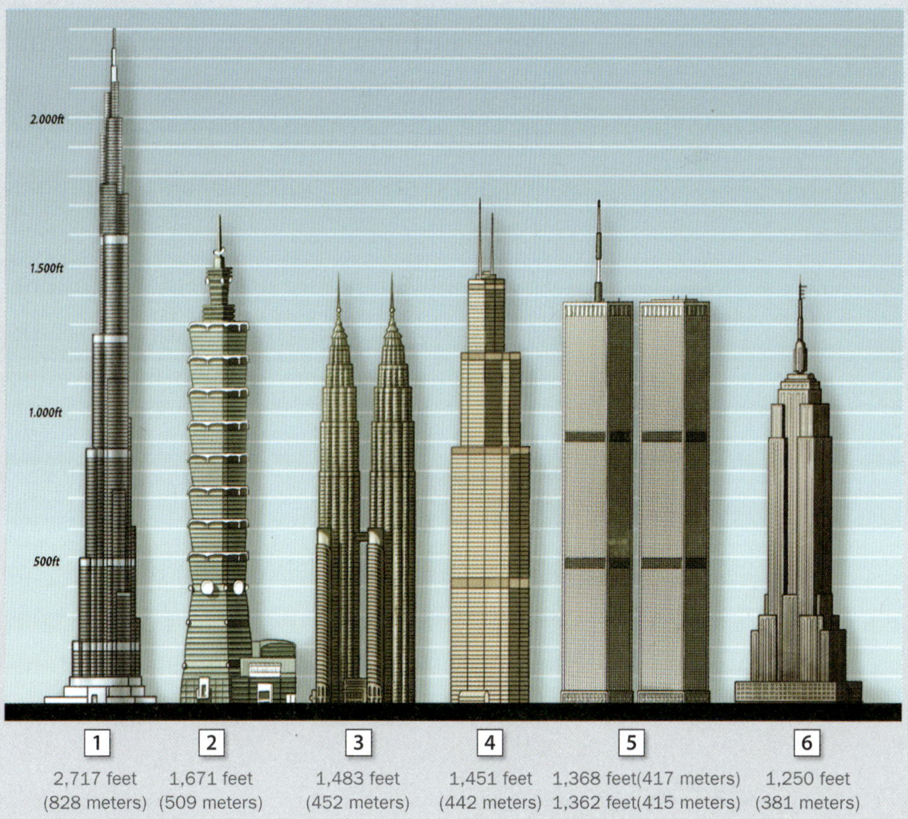

UNIT 15

The Big Question

What primary component enabled the rapid proliferation of skyscrapers?

The Birth of the Skyscraper

16

► Notes

The first **skyscraper** was the ten-story Home Insurance Building, completed in Chicago in 1885. Though a building of such stature would likely fail to impress anyone today, both its height and structure were revolutionary at the time, ushering in an age of **vertical** urban growth.

Before the mid-1800s, buildings utilized load-bearing **masonry** walls, made out of brick or stone, to support the weight of their upper floors. The taller a building, the more weight its lower walls had to bear, and the thicker they needed to be. This imposed a relatively strict limit on building height—anything taller than six stories would **necessitate** load-bearing walls so thick they would **impede** any use of the building's interior. Yet, during the latter half of the 19th century, city planners were demanding more and more tall buildings as populations swelled and available urban space became scarcer.

The solution came from a new building material: steel. Steel weighed less, allowed for more flexibility, could support more weight, and was far less bulky than masonry walls. Tall, grid-like frameworks were fashioned using steel, and these functioned as the "**skeletons**" of buildings, on which thin, light-weight concrete and glass walls were hung. Whereas in traditional construction walls played an essential structural role, in these new buildings they served simply to keep out the elements and let in light. It was this **manner** of steel-frame construction that made possible Chicago's Home Insurance Building and the hundreds of much taller skyscrapers that followed it.

skyscraper a tall commercial building
vertical positioned at an angle of 90° to the horizon
masonry stone or brick structures
necessitate to make necessary or essential
impede to be an obstacle

Of course, people also needed a method for reaching these **towering** structures. Steam-powered elevators had been in use for several years, but the public did not consider them safe, for if the cable that lifted and lowered the elevator broke, the **compartment** would plummet and crash at the ground floor. A man named Elisha Graves Otis **addressed** this concern with the invention of the Otis safety elevator, which featured a braking system that, if a cable broke and the elevator started to descend out of control, would halt the fall of the elevator box. Soon, the "Otis safety" became a standard element of this new generation of tall buildings.

Once all of the components to make the construction of skyscrapers feasible were in place, they began to take over city skylines at a rapid pace. New York quickly transformed into a home for the tallest buildings in the world, including the Chrysler Building in 1930 and the Empire State Building in 1931. Ever since, the world's metropolises have been engaged in something of a competition to possess the highest skyscraper, and in 2010 Dubai claimed the title with its 2,717-foot Burj Khalifa, far outstripping the previous record holder, Taiwan's Taipei 101 at 1,671 feet. Throughout the world, the skyscraper serves to define cities and will continue to do so for the foreseeable future.

► Notes

▲ Load-bearing masonry walls

On Your Own

What is the tallest building you have ever been in? What was it like?

skeleton internal structure that provides support
manner way of doing something
towering reaching a great height
compartment a small enclosed space
address to turn one's attention to or deal with something

Vocabulary Building

[1-6] Complete each sentence with one of the words from the box.

flexibility / once / available / bulky / impose / defines

1. We'd prefer to be seated next to one another if there is a pairs of seats ______________.

2. Due to its ______________, the suspension bridge swayed and undulated dangerously.

3. My blue bathrobe is too ______________ to fit into my suitcase.

4. The road is scheduled to open ______________ it has been declared safe for vehicles.

5. With its distinctive shape, the Harbour Centre Tower ______________ Vancouver's skyline.

6. European invaders attempted to ______________ their culture upon Latin America.

[7-12] Choose the words that are closest in meaning to the underlined ones.

7. These steel beams must be strong enough to <u>bear</u> the weight of the porch roof.

a. trim　b. contain　c. construct　d. support

8. Bears are most attracted to human campsites when food is <u>scarce</u>.

a. necessary　b. rare　c. defined　d. favored

9. According to a recent report, beautiful artwork, like music, <u>functions</u> as a painkiller.

a. acts　b. disguises　c. originates　d. stands

10. A very tall person may have to <u>lower</u> his or her head to pass through the door frame.

a. drop　b. twist　c. raise　d. strain

11. The researchers <u>descended</u> into the cave to explore its strange, isolated ecosystem.

a. entered　b. went down　c. passed　d. extended

12. The sky blackened and the clouds began to <u>swell</u> just before the big storm.

a. move　b. grow　c. threaten　d. retreat

[13-15] Complete each sentence with the following idioms.

in place / keep out / out of control

13. The car went completely ________________, injuring five people.

14. All of the actors need to be ________________ five minutes before the curtain opens.

15. We need to put screens on our windows in the summer to ________________ the bugs.

Reading Comprehension

1 What is the main idea of the passage?

a. Skyscrapers have changed relatively little over the years.
b. Today's skyscrapers are not as sturdy as those built using masonry walls.
c. New York City has always been home to the tallest buildings in the world.
d. Construction innovations in the 1800s led to skyscrapers becoming widespread.

2 What was the significance of the Otis safety elevator?

a. It was the first elevator mechanism to be used inside a building.
b. It pioneered the use of steel cables in skyscraper construction.
c. It provided a secure way of moving within a skyscraper.
d. It influenced the design of Chicago's Home Insurance Building.

3 Why were masonry walls impractical for use in tall buildings?

a. They needed to be extremely wide.
b. They became too thick when used in tall buildings.
c. They were time consuming to build.
d. They were made from expensive materials.

4 The word outstripping in the passage is closest in meaning to

a. following   b. measuring
c. beating   d. calling

5 Which of the following was NOT a component of early skyscrapers?

a. the Otis safety elevator
b. thin walls of concrete and glass
c. an internal "skeleton" made of steel
d. thick stone walls at the building's base

6 What can be inferred about the Home Insurance Building?

a. It has been preserved as a historical landmark.
b. It did not possess an elevator.
c. It was an object of wonder to people in 1885.
d. It was added onto to become taller in later years.

7 What makes steel such a good construction material?

8 Why were skyscrapers in demand during the late 1800s?

9 Currently, what is the world's tallest building and where is it?

Summary

Step 1 **Read the passage again and complete the outline with the words below.**

six / constructed / unsafe / less / steel / skylines
masonry walls / elevator / skyscraper / brakes / New York / tallest

I. Buildings before mid-1800s

A. Relied on ____________ to support weight

B. Limited to ____________ floors due to size requirements of lower walls

II. Introduction of ____________

A. Steel frameworks weighed ____________, were smaller, and could support more weight

B. Home Insurance Building ____________ in 1885

III. Otis safety ____________

A. Previous elevators were considered ____________

B. Otis added safety ____________ and produced a viable elevator for skyscrapers

IV. Age of the ____________

A. The city of ____________ was home to many of the first major skyscrapers

B. City ____________ around the world began to be dominated by skyscrapers

C. Cities now compete to have the ____________ building in the world

Step 2 **Complete the summary with your own words based on the outline.**

Prior to the mid-1800s, buildings relied on ____________ to support the weight of their upper floors. ____________

____

____

____

____

____

____________ Cities now compete to have the ____________ building in the world.

Unit 16: The Placebo Effect

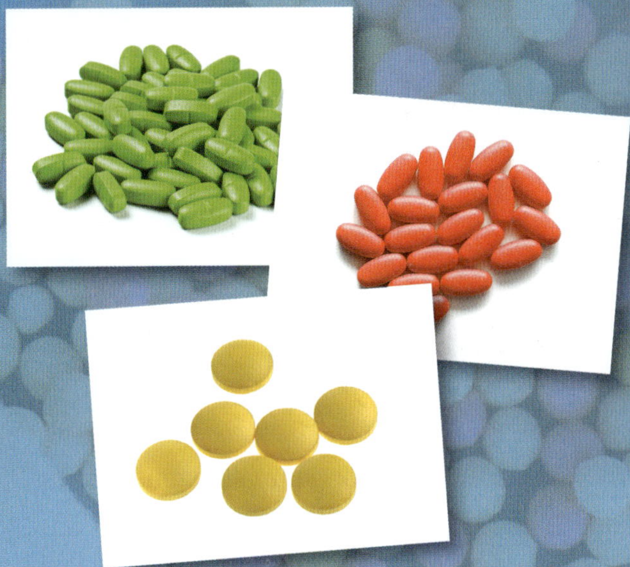

Getting Started

1 Look at the pictures. Which pills do you think would be effective and why?

2 Have you heard of the placebo effect? If you have, could you explain what it is? If you haven't, can you guess what it is?

3 What if a doctor gave you candy, but told you it was medicine? Do you think it would still make you feel better?

Building Background Knowledge

Clinical Trials

Clinical trials are health-related studies in humans conducted by teams of health care professionals and researchers. Participants are volunteers who want to try new research treatments or contribute to medical research. Volunteers are selected based on factors such as age, gender, medical condition, and previous treatment history. Some clinical trials need healthy participants while others look for volunteers with certain illnesses or conditions that they can study.

Each participant must sign an informed consent form before the study can begin. In order to get informed consent, the staff must make sure individuals are aware of the key facts concerning the clinical trial and the risks and benefits of participating in it. The prospective volunteer must also be mentally healthy enough to make decisions for himself or herself before agreeing to get involved.

In a typical clinical trial, researchers divide participants into two groups. One group of participants is given an experimental medication or treatment and the other is given a placebo. The research team can compare the results of the two groups in order to determine the effectiveness of the experimental treatment.

UNIT 16

The Placebo Effect

17

The Big Question

What is the placebo effect?

▸ Notes

A placebo is an **inert** medical treatment that generally comes in the form of a sugar pill but can also be any 'dummy treatment' such as an injection of a **saline solution**, a special diet or exercise program, or 'fake' surgery. Placebos were discovered in the 18th century and have fascinated the medical world for their uncanny ability to heal. In fact, one third of the people who take placebos for illnesses experience relief from their symptoms, a phenomenon known as "the placebo effect."

Doctors are still unsure how exactly placebos work; however, they have learned that certain factors greatly influence the outcome of a placebo treatment. **Skepticism**, for example, often hinders the positive results of a placebo. A poor relationship between a patient and his or her doctor can do the same. On the other hand, those who trust their health care practitioners are more likely to have a beneficial outcome. Additionally, research shows that the characteristics, such as the color and design, of a placebo pill are more powerful than the pills themselves. Yellow pills have proven the most effective in treating depression; patients find red pills more stimulating; and green pills are the most helpful in reducing anxiety. Sugar pills that resemble widely recognized drugs are also more effective than **generic** ones.

There are several theories that attempt to explain why the placebo effect works. One idea is that a person's expectations of certain improvements are powerful enough to bring about the desired results. Others believe that the placebo effect is merely coincidence, as many

inert having no drug-like effect
saline solution salt water
skepticism the state of not believing
generic not having a brand name or manufacturer
disorder a physical or mental problem

disorders treated with placebos are self-limiting, meaning that they will heal themselves naturally over a certain period of time. Some theorists suggest that taking a placebo may motivate people to take better care of themselves or reduce their fears and anxieties, explaining any improvements they may experience. Another theory says that the act of taking a placebo could also cause a patient to re-evaluate their symptoms as less severe.

▸ Notes

Placebos have been known to cause certain **side effects**, including **nausea**, **drowsiness**, and skin **rashes**. In some cases, doctors have seen their patients become dependant on placebos, believing that they will fall ill as soon as they stop taking them. In other cases, patients who are convinced that a treatment will produce undesirable consequences may come to experience the feared symptoms. This phenomenon is called "the nocebo effect." Healthy individuals who are **prescribed** placebos over a long period of time can also become convinced that they are indeed sick, triggering the onset of genuine symptoms.

Despite their potential unwanted side effects, placebos are vital to clinical trials where researchers must determine the effectiveness of a new drug. They do this by comparing the results of their potential product with those of a placebo. The new drug may receive government approval in countries like the United States only if it generates better results than a placebo. According to the U.S. Food and Drug Administration (FDA), half of all new drugs fail to beat a placebo in the required clinical trials.

On Your Own

Have you ever felt better or worse about something just by thinking about it?

side effect a negative accompanying effect of a drug
nausea the state of being sick to the stomach and feeling the need to vomit
drowsiness the state of being sleepy
rash irritation of the skin
prescribe to specify a treatment for a patient

Vocabulary Building

[1-8] Complete each sentence with one of the words from the box.

approval / phenomenon / undesirable / coincidence
uncanny / stimulating / fascinate / treat

1. My grandmother has the ______________ ability to perceive exactly what's bothering me before I tell her.

2. The museum has plenty of exhibits that will surely ______________ the kids in your class.

3. Its huge popularity turned the television show into a Canadian ______________.

4. You may be able to ______________ your anxiety with meditation and mental exercises.

5. Black tea has a(n) ______________ effect while chamomile has a soothing one.

6. It was a strange ______________ that I ran into two old college friends in one day.

7. I wish that I were more outgoing; being shy is a(n) ______________ trait.

8. Before we sign the contract, I will need to get ______________ from my manager.

[9-15] Choose the words that are closest in meaning to the underlined ones.

9. I feared that the noise outside my tent was a bear, but it was <u>merely</u> a squirrel.
a. surprisingly b. at last c. fortunately d. just

10. He <u>convinced</u> me to go to the party even though I had homework to do.
a. prevented b. persuaded c. doubted d. instructed

11. The company worries that climate regulations will <u>hinder</u> future growth.
a. enforce b. deny c. reverse d. prevent

12. We won't know the <u>outcome</u> of the tournament until after the final match.
a. result b. process c. schedule d. acceptability

13. Signing up for a fun dance class may <u>motivate</u> you to exercise.
a. inspire b. deceive c. allow d. analyze

14. The wool in this scarf may <u>trigger</u> an allergic reaction in people with sensitive skin.
a. permit b. calm c. suspect d. initiate

15. From a distance, it's hard to tell if this is a <u>genuine</u> luxury item or a fake.
a. foreign b. clean c. real d. functional

Reading Comprehension

1 What is the main idea of the passage?

a. The nocebo effect cancels out the medical benefits of the placebo effect.
b. The act of getting help may be enough to cure people of some illnesses.
c. Placebos may cause various side effects in patients.
d. Most medical practitioners rely on placebos to cure their patients.

2 Which of the following treatments would be considered a placebo?

a. drugs prescribed by a doctor
b. an FDA approved medication
c. an injection of saline solution
d. cosmetic surgery procedures

3 What is a self-limiting disorder?

a. a condition that can be treated with a placebo
b. a type of disease that is studied in clinical trials
c. a sickness that does not respond to medication
d. an illness that will heal itself naturally

4 The word onset in the passage is closest in meaning to

a. origin b. start
c. delay d. capacity

5 Which of the following is NOT a possible explanation of why the placebo effect works?

a. Patients often take better care of themselves while taking placebos.
b. Placebos provide an artificial boost to the body's immune system.
c. Placebo treatments help relieve stress and calm people's fears.
d. People taking placebos may interpret their symptoms differently.

6 What can be inferred about new drugs developed in the United States?

a. Around half receive approval from the FDA after beating the placebo test.
b. Many are simply placebos with no chemically active ingredients.
c. Few cause the same kind of unwanted side effects that placebos do.
d. Most evolved from traditional placebos administered for centuries.

7 What are some factors that influence the effectiveness of a placebo treatment?

8 What is "the nocebo effect"?

9 How can a new drug receive approval from the U.S. Food and Drug Administration?

Summary

Step 1 **Read the passage again and complete the outline with the words below.**

inert / skepticism / color / negative / treatment / influences
sugar / theories / diseases / the nocebo effect / side effects / clinical

I. The placebo effect

A. Relief that sick patients feel from ____________ medical treatments

B. Placebos: ____________ pills, saline injections, other dummy treatments

II. ____________ on outcome

A. ____________ and poor doctor-patient relationship lower success rate

B. ____________ associations and believability of pill design can improve results

III. ____________ behind the placebo effect

A. People's beliefs/expectations can affect the outcome of a ____________

B. ____________ heal themselves naturally

IV. ____________ aspects

A. ____________, dependency

B. ____________: fear of negative effects may produce them

V. ____________ trials

A. Used to test effectiveness of new drugs

Step 2 **Complete the summary with your own words based on the outline.**

The placebo effect is relief that sick patients feel from ____________ medical treatments.
____
____
____
____
____ Placebos are necessary in ____________ trials, where they are used to test the effectiveness of new drugs.

Part IV

• Content Area : Economics

Unit 17: Greenwashing

Getting Started

1. Which gift do you think looks more environmentally friendly and why?
2. What do you pay attention to when comparing product brands?
3. Are you willing to buy organic food even if it costs more? Why or why not?

Building Background Knowledge

Third-Party Certification

Green marketing is the practice of making "green" claims about products and services in order to cater to a new generation of environmentally concerned customers. An important step in the green marketing process is getting third-party certification. Since there are currently no global manufacturing standards for companies to follow, third-party certification is the only way for customers to verify which products are truly environmentally friendly and which are not.

▲ USDA (U.S. Department of Agriculture) organic certification

Third-party certification can come from any reputable, unbiased independent organization that is devoted to ensuring that certain ecological standards are being met. A third party requires a company to disclose all the ingredients it uses in a product and then conducts independent laboratory tests to check if the claims the company is making about that product are true. If their test results match the company's environmental claims, they will award the company with written certification that it can proudly advertise on its product packaging or in advertising campaigns.

UNIT 17

Greenwashing

18

The Big Question

What is the intended purpose of greenwashing?

► Notes

The late 1980s saw the **advent** of new **trends** in environmentalism and corporate social responsibility, which led to the birth of green marketing. Companies realized that customers were becoming more **ecologically** concerned, which ultimately affected their shopping habits. It seemed natural, then, for businesses to adjust their marketing processes so that there was more focus on the **environmentally friendly** aspects of their products or services. Green marketing proved to be so successful, however, that many businesses started adopting green marketing practices in order to sell products that were not really good for the environment.

This practice of falsely advertising products or services as environmentally friendly is called "greenwashing" and it is widely used across the globe. Some companies have turned to greenwashing because it is the easiest and least expensive way to satisfy customers demanding ecologically friendly products. Others do it to compete with competitor companies that have already jumped on the "go green" bandwagon or to prevent government bodies or environmentalists from criticizing their business practices. Many times, the exaggerated environmental claims of companies are intentional, while other times they can be the result of ignorance or **sloppy** marketing.

One of the most effective tricks of the advertising trade is to play with a product's **packaging** design, and this is often done in greenwashing practices as well. Green, blue, and white have turned into popular color choices for companies wanting to promote the environmental benefits of

advent the beginning of something
trend something popular at a given time
ecologically in a manner related to nature
environmentally friendly not causing harm to nature
sloppy unorganized and of poor quality

their products. **Hemp** sacks and recycled brown paper wrapping, along with pictures of the globe, clear skies, and growing grass, are used to convince customers that the product they are about to purchase will not harm the earth. But the line between green marketing and greenwashing can be hard to discern: These smart packaging designs do not necessarily mean that the product they contain is environmentally friendly.

Examples of greenwashing can be found in almost every industry. A classic example is a hotel chain that claims to care about the environment because it asks guests to consider reusing their towels and bed sheets. While this practice does indeed save water and energy, the hotel chain is not truly green unless it is implementing similar energy-conservation practices elsewhere. The water and energy saved from reused towels does not make up for excessive electricity, heat, air conditioning, or overall water usage. In fact, one of the biggest **motivators** for hotels to ask customers to reuse their towels and bed sheets is simply to save money.

As greenwashing becomes more and more common, it is hard for customers to know exactly who they can trust. Products to look out for include those that claim to be green without providing any proof. Truly green products are generally backed by a third-party **certification**. Customers should also be wary of products that use vague key words like "all-natural," "earth smart," or "environmentally safe" to get their attention. These terms are not recognized as meaningful by any government or third-party organization. As a smart consumer, it is essential that you do your research before making any **purchases**. Despite the companies who greenwash, there are still a good number of businesses that have truly taken on the cause of conservation.

▲ "Green" packaging design

► Notes

On Your Own

Are there any truly environmentally friendly products in your home? What are they?

packaging the material in which something is wrapped
hemp a type of plant that is used to make rope and strong rough cloth
motivator something that makes you want to achieve something
certification official validation
purchase the act of buying something

Vocabulary Building

[1-6] Complete each sentence with one of the words from the box.

conservation / implement / falsely / ignorance / chain / practice

1. His ____________ of proper table manners caused me much embarrassment.

2. The ____________ of donating blood is common in Europe and North America.

3. Environmentalists promote the ____________ of natural resources.

4. John's jealous classmate ____________ accused him of cheating on the exam.

5. The fast-food ____________ was criticized for its unhealthy menu.

6. The company will ____________ its new business plan next month.

[7-12] Choose the words that are closest in meaning to the underlined ones.

7. Sometimes it's difficult to <u>discern</u> fake designer brands from real ones.
a. afford b. detect c. explain d. purchase

8. <u>Excessive</u> sweating after exercise could be a sign of illness.
a. too much b. moderate c. unexplained d. guarded

9. Joanne's insult wasn't <u>intentional</u>, so I didn't get angry at her.
a. severe b. humorous c. understandable d. calculated

10. You should be <u>wary</u> of salespeople who speak very quickly.
a. unwelcome b. sympathetic c. cautious d. aggressive

11. The team performed poorly at first but <u>ultimately</u> won the game.
a. initially b. wisely c. unfortunately d. finally

12. Just as my brother had claimed, there was <u>indeed</u> a stranger at the door.
a. actually b. oddly c. typically d. fortunately

[13-15] Complete each sentence with the following idioms.

jump on the bandwagon / look out for / take on

13. Evan didn't understand why cell phones were so popular but he decided to ________________ and buy one anyway.

14. This year I ________________ the challenge of running for class president.

15. When hiking in the mountains, ________________ falling rocks.

Reading Comprehension

1 What is the main idea of the passage?

a. Companies that engage in greenwashing should be fined.
b. Greenwashing is a modern variety of false advertising.
c. Most products sold today are not good for the environment.
d. Green marketing is more prevalent than greenwashing.

2 What led to the development of greenwashing?

a. increased consumer demand for ecologically conscious products
b. government mandates that products meet certain environmental goals
c. competition in the green market from international companies
d. unintentional errors in the marketing practices of some firms

3 According to the passage, how do some hotels participate in greenwashing?

a. by cutting down on heating and air-conditioning
b. by painting the exteriors of their buildings green
c. by encouraging guests to reuse towels and sheets
d. by using less water in their day-to-day operations

4 The word exaggerated in the passage is closest in meaning to

a. inspected　　b. overstated
c. anticipated　　d. renowned

5 Which of the following is NOT mentioned in the passage as a packaging element used in greenwashing?

a. images of skies and grass　　b. recycled wrapping materials
c. colors like blue and white　　d. false certification information

6 What can be inferred about the terms "all-natural," "earth smart," and "environmentally safe"?

a. They are reserved for use in hotels.
b. They were not used before the introduction of greenwashing.
c. They symbolize different levels of certification.
d. They represent a greenwashing tactic.

7 What is the aim of green marketing?

8 What are two reasons that companies engage in greenwashing?

9 How do consumers know when a product is truly good for the environment?

Summary

Step 1 **Read the passage again and complete the outline with the words below.**

greenwashing / companies / package / government / green marketing
environment / smart / colors / hotels / reuse / compete / third-party / conservation

I. The rise of ____________

A. Consumer concern for the ____________ increased in the late 1980s

B. ____________ success led to false advertising, or greenwashing

II. Why ____________ greenwash

A. To ____________ with green competitors

B. To prevent the ____________ from criticizing their business practices

III. Greenwashing in ____________ design

A. ____________ packaging is an old advertising tool

B. Greenwashed packaging features specific ____________, images, and materials

IV. Greenwashing in ____________

A. Guests asked to ____________ towels and sheets so hotels can save money

B. Real environmentalism demands stronger ____________ action

V. Spotting and avoiding greenwashing

A. Look for ____________ certification **B.** Conduct research to verify marketing claims

Step 2 **Complete the summary with your own words based on the outline.**

The history of ____________ can be traced back to the late 1980s, when consumers started demonstrating an increased concern for the ____________. ____________
____
____
____
____ In order to spot and avoid greenwashing, consumers should look for ____________ certification on products. Also, they must conduct research to verify marketing claims.

Unit 18: Predicting Volcanic Eruptions

Getting Started

1. Look at the picture. Can you guess why there is heavy smoke?
2. Do you know why volcanoes erupt?
3. How can we predict volcanic eruptions?

Building Background Knowledge

Colombian Volcano, Nevado Del Ruiz

Volcanoes are highly unpredictable, and a sudden eruption or burst of geological activity can have devastating consequences. This is why it is essential for authorities to have effective civil emergency procedures in place to help protect those living near volcanoes.

One tragic example of the importance of this type of emergency planning occurred in the shadow of the Colombian volcano Nevado del Ruiz in 1985. The residents of the small town of Armero were completely unprepared for any kind of natural disaster, despite the fact that the settlement had originally been established on the site of a deadly 19th-century *lahar*, or volcanic mudflow. When a minor eruption of Nevado del Ruiz generated another *lahar* that raced downhill towards the town, there was no warning system to alert the residents about the danger. As a result, around 90 percent of Armero's 27,000 residents were killed and the town itself was completely wiped out.

UNIT 18

The Big Question

How are volcanic eruptions predicted?

Predicting Volcanic Eruptions

► Notes

Throughout history, somewhere around 500 volcanic eruptions have been recorded on planet Earth and scientists estimate that there are about 1,500 potentially active volcanoes in existence today, excluding those on the ocean floor. Approximately 500 million people live near an active volcano and many are unaware of the potential danger they are in. In the past, trying to figure out when a volcano would **erupt** was more or less a guessing game; however, although not an exact science, volcanologists are now able to more accurately predict volcanic eruptions thanks to three reliable techniques: **seismic** monitoring, gas monitoring, and ground **deformation** studies.

Seismic monitoring is the measurement of ground motion, which can tip volcanologists off about an impending eruption. Also used to detect earthquakes, seismographs are capable of identifying the shifting of rock in the Earth's **crust**, which may be the result of rising magma, or liquid **molten rock**, in an agitated volcano. During the beginning stage of an eruption, internal gas pressure inside a volcano causes magma to rise to the surface, breaking rock along the way. Using seismographs, data of these **ruptures** is collected and transmitted via radio to computer-equipped monitoring stations, where scientists can keep an eye out for abnormal behavior far from the volcano's danger zone.

A second, equally important technique used for predicting volcanic eruptions is the monitoring of gas emissions at the mouth of a volcano. When magma bubbles to the surface just before an explosion, it releases

erupt to eject molten rock, ash, and gas from a volcano
seismic relating to the vibration of the Earth
deformation changes in Earth's crust resulting from geologic processes
crust the rocky outer layer of the Earth
molten rock rock under the Earth's surface that has been heated to its melting point

extremely large quantities of **sulfur dioxide** into the air. Previously, it was necessary for volcanologists to crawl into the **crater** of a volcano in order to record the quantities of the gases being emitted; however, scientists are currently developing new tools such as **infrared telescopes** that can transmit gas emission data automatically and continuously from a volcanic crater to a laboratory so that vital warning signs may be registered without putting human lives in danger.

▸ Notes

It is also valuable to study ground deformation, or the change in a volcano's shape or positioning, because such movement can be an indicator of magma rising to the surface. Sensitive tools like **tiltmeters** and surveying instruments can detect minute changes below the surface of a volcano, which volcanologists use to estimate the depth of a magma source, as well as how fast the magma is traveling to the surface. As with gas monitoring, ground deformation studies used to require humans to climb dangerously close to the mouth of a volcano until the invention of global positioning system satellites that allow for the constant and continuous transmission of ground deformation data to remote observatories.

While volcanic eruptions can be predicted using seismic monitoring, gas monitoring, and deformation studies, scientific method is unable to tell us exactly how large or serious an eruption will be. Furthermore, even with the combined use of sensitive monitoring techniques, each volcano's eruptive behavior is unique and ever-changing. Volcanologists must therefore be aware of a volcano's complete history if they hope to understand anything about the type, direction, or magnitude of its future eruptions.

On Your Own

How should people prepare for a volcanic eruption?

rupture a state of being broken
sulfur dioxide a toxic gas emitted by a volcano
crater a hole at the opening of a volcano
infrared telescope a telescope that detects heat
tiltmeter a tool that measures small changes in the slope of Earth's crust

Vocabulary Building

[1-6] Complete each sentence with one of the words from the box.

indicator / remote / estimate / transmit / crawl / release

1. This fish will ____________ a toxin into the water when it feels threatened.

2. The satellite will take photos of space and ____________ them back to Earth.

3. Sensitive data is stored in ____________ research facilities, far from harm.

4. Babies learn to ____________ on their hands and knees before they learn to walk.

5. The monthly sales report is a good ____________ of how well business is doing.

6. I don't know exact value of the house but I can give you a pretty good ____________.

[7-12] Choose the words that are closest in meaning to the underlined ones.

7. It is believed that the worldwide population of wild Giant Pandas is <u>approximately</u> 1,500.
a. at least b. realistically c. significantly d. around

8. <u>Minute</u> changes in the atmosphere are difficult to notice without sensitive equipment.
a. simple b. tiny c. evident d. measured

9. An earthquake with a <u>magnitude</u> of less than 3.0 does not usually cause much damage.
a. duration b. location c. intensity d. frequency

10. She agreed to the plan, but I could <u>detect</u> a trace of hesitation in her voice.
a. sense b. generate c. predict d. imagine

11. A house pet may be sick or in pain if it exhibits <u>abnormal</u> behavior.
a. unusual b. ordinary c. receptive d. fearful

12. Some deep sea creatures <u>emit</u> light to attract mates or prey.
a. reproduce b. trace c. give off d. concentrate

[13-15] Complete each sentence with the following idioms.

thanks to / keep an eye out for / figure out

13. It only takes me five minutes to ________________ how a movie will end.

14. I was able to pay my university tuition ________________ a government grant.

15. She stood by the window to ________________ her sister, who was on her way.

Reading Comprehension

1 What is the passage mainly about?

a. threats volcanoes pose to nearby residents
b. methods of forecasting a volcanic eruption
c. the importance of recording ground motion
d. historical occurrences of volcanic eruptions

2 Why is it helpful for scientists to know an individual volcano's history?

a. It gives them clues about when other volcanoes will erupt.
b. It allows them to develop precise models of volcanic activity.
c. It aids in their understanding of a volcano's unique behavior.
d. It tells them the precise size of a volcano's future eruptions.

3 What can be monitored by an infrared telescope?

a. ground motion
b. gas emission
c. ground deformation
d. magma speed

4 The word impending in the passage is closest in meaning to

a. interfering
b. forthcoming
c. resisting
d. noticeable

5 Which is NOT mentioned as a sign of a volcanic eruption?

a. seismic motion of the ground
b. large quantities of gas emission
c. magma rising to the surface
d. a sudden increase of volcanic craters

6 What can be inferred about the process involved in collecting ground deformation data?

a. It is regarded as an inexact science.
b. It no longer endangers human lives.
c. It requires the same tools used in gas monitoring.
d. It is more difficult than other detection methods.

7 What can seismic monitoring tell volcanologists?

8 What kind of gas do volcanologists look for when trying to predict an eruption?

9 How are the small changes in the ground below a volcano detected?

Summary

Step 1 **Read the passage again and complete the outline with the words below.**

volcanoes / seismic / motion / gas / deformation / magma
erupt / active / mouth / shape / sulfur dioxide

I. ______________

A. 1,500 potentially ______________ volcanoes around the world

B. ______________ monitoring, gas monitoring, and ground deformation studies predict when they will ______________

II. **Seismic monitoring**

A. Measurement of ground ______________ with seismographs

III. ______________ **monitoring**

A. Study of gases emitted from volcano's ______________

B. ______________ indicates magma bubbling to surface before an eruption

IV. **Ground ______________ studies**

A. Study of changes in a volcano's ______________ or positioning

B. Movements indicate ______________ rising to the surface

Step 2 **Complete the summary with your own words based on the outline.**

There are 1,500 potentially ______________ volcanoes around the world. ______________
____
____
____
____
____
____
______________ Any movements indicate ______________ rising to the surface.

Unit 19: A Star is Born

Getting Started

1. Look at the picture. What do you see?
2. Can you guess how they were created?
3. What do you know about space?

Building Background Knowledge

Black Holes

A black hole is an area in space where the force of gravity is so strong that it sucks up anything that enters it. The superior strength of gravity in a black hole comes from a dense amount of matter that is crammed inside an extremely small space. This can result from the collapse of a giant star in its final stages of life. Once any form of matter is sucked into a black hole, it is doomed to remain trapped there forever. Even light, which can travel at a speed of 186,284 miles (299,792 kilometers) per second, is unable to escape from a black hole, thus making a black hole appear black.

Scientists have a difficult time studying black holes because they cannot be seen, heard, or explored. However, powerful telescopes allow scientists to observe how black holes affect other celestial bodies. Based on calculations of radiation that is emitted when matter is swallowed up into a black hole, it is believed that a large number of black holes exist in the universe.

UNIT 19

A Star is Born

The Big Question

What is a star made of?

► Notes

There are hundreds of billions of stars in our **galaxy**, the Milky Way. Each one is unique and has a life of its own. Stars have life cycles like humans and other living **creatures**. They are born, live, and then die. Unlike humans, though, stars do not have parents. Instead, they are born through a fascinating process.

All the elements must be right for a star to be born. Our galaxy contains enormous clouds of gas and **dust** called nebulae. More specifically, nebulae consist of leftover parts of old stars, lots of hydrogen, and a little bit of helium. A nebula has the potential to become a star, as well as an **asteroid** or a planet. However, before it can become a star, it must first become a protostar. When gravity pulls a cloud of gas and dust together, it contracts into a dense ball with a very hot center. This dense ball is called a protostar, and it is the beginning stage of a star's life.

As the protostar heats up, the pressure builds on the energy **particles**, or atoms. The heavier elements of the protostar are pushed to its core and the lighter elements, such as hydrogen and helium, move to its surface. Eventually, a protostar will reach the incredible temperature of 15 million degrees Celsius. When this happens, the nuclei, or center part of the atoms, start to smash into one another. The impact is so hard that the nuclei stick together. This process is called nuclear **fusion**, and it keeps the protostar from falling apart under the pressure of gravity. Nuclear fusion also causes the hydrogen and helium gases to catch on fire, creating a new brightly glowing star.

galaxy a cluster of stars held together by gravity
creature a living being (usually other than a human)
dust a cloud of small, fine particles
asteroid a small planet that orbits the sun especially between Mars and Jupiter
particle a small component of matter

Like humans, stars go through many changes throughout their lifetime. After burning its hydrogen for millions or billions of years, a star reaches the middle of its life. A star without much **mass** will not glow as brightly or be as hot as a star that was made with more gas and dust. Stars with more mass also have a larger supply of hydrogen and can burn longer. Eventually, every star will completely run out of hydrogen and lose the ability to glow. At this point, the star will begin to cool down and expand. When all that is left is helium, the star will become bright red and transform into a glowing red giant.

▸ Notes

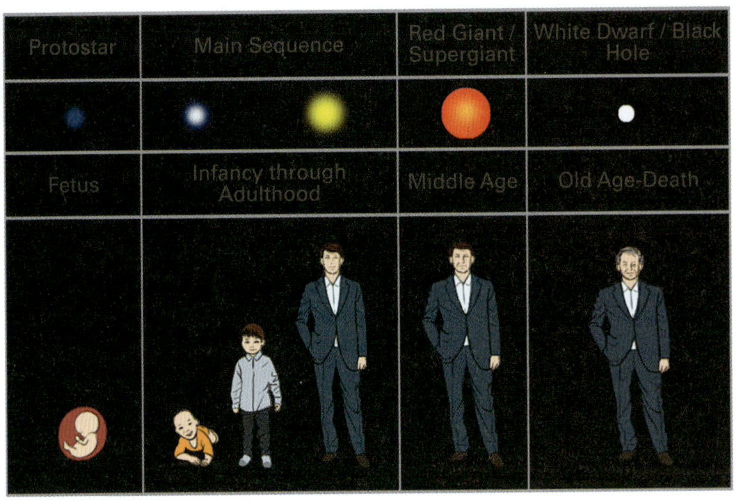

Red giants can take one of two paths. Medium-sized stars, like our Sun, turn into white dwarves that burn until their helium supply is gone. Then, they turn inside themselves and die, becoming black **dwarves**. Massive stars, on the other hand, take another route. A massive red giant gets hotter and hotter until it generates a supernova, which is a massive **stellar** explosion that can get as hot as 1,000,000,000 degrees Celsius and light up the sky for several months. Then, the **void** left behind after the explosion is swallowed up by gravity and a black hole is formed.

On Your Own

What do you know about stars?

fusion in physics, a reaction in which atoms join
mass in physics, the property of matter which results in it having weight
dwarf in astronomy, a small star of average brightness
stellar relating to stars
void an empty area of space where nothing exists

Vocabulary Building

[1-6] Complete each sentence with one of the words from the box.

element / contract / leftover / dense / expand / reaction

1. If there is any ____________ food from dinner tonight, I'll have it for lunch tomorrow.

2. By unzipping these sections, you can ____________ the bag so it'll fit more clothes.

3. When our body is exposed to cold, muscles ____________ or shiver to make heat.

4. I scooped up several handfuls of snow and packed them into a ____________ snowball.

5. Mixing baking soda and vinegar will produce a frothy chemical ____________.

6. Hydrogen is both the lightest and the most abundant ____________ in the universe.

[7-12] Choose the words that are closest in meaning to the underlined ones.

7. Call a friend for support before you <u>reach</u> the point of hopelessness.
a. remember b. develop c. attain d. inspire

8. The squirrel shook the birdfeeder for a while but <u>eventually</u> gave up and went away.
a. peacefully b. reluctantly c. finally d. complexly

9. In between the surface of the Earth and its <u>core</u> lies a region called the mantle.
a. center b. soil c. shell d. mountains

10. We dropped a watermelon from the roof and watched it <u>smash</u> onto the pavement.
a. sneak b. hold c. rebound d. crash

11. Pine trees contain gummy sap that can <u>stick</u> to your hands for days.
a. adhere b. station c. gush d. accelerate

12. Cars on the Autobahn travel at <u>incredible</u> speeds since there is no speed limit.
a. secondary b. audible c. unbelievable d. ultimate

[13-15] Complete each sentence with the following idioms.

run out of / fall apart / go through

13. Our old barn finally ________________ after a huge snowstorm this month.

14. You can't ________________ an experience like that without being affected by it.

15. Sharon was planning to bake cookies for the surprise party, but she ________________ flour.

Reading Comprehension

1 What is the main idea of the passage?

a. Stars significantly influence the formation of asteroids.
b. The complexity of a star cannot be understood by humans.
c. Stars go through many changes during their lifetime.
d. The human life cycle is more advanced than that of stars.

2 What must a star fight against in order to stay alive?

a. nuclei
b. gravity
c. oxygen
d. atoms

3 What happens to a star when it runs out of hydrogen?

a. It will lose the ability to burn brightly.
b. It will be born again as a glowing red giant.
c. It will shrivel up and turn into a black dwarf.
d. It will condense and expand infinitely.

4 The word potential in the passage is closest in meaning to

a. experience
b. ability
c. elegance
d. quantity

5 Which of the following is NOT mentioned in the passage as part of a star's life cycle?

a. Nuclear fusion occurs and it makes a star glow.
b. A star runs out of hydrogen at the end of its life.
c. Gravity transforms a nebula into a protostar.
d. Medium-sized stars generate enormous supernovas.

6 What can be inferred about a star's lifespan?

a. The longevity of a star is determined by its mass.
b. Stars are born, die and then are reborn in an endless cycle.
c. A star's lifespan depends on its proximity to other stars.
d. Cooler temperatures ensure that stars live longer.

7 How are stars formed?

8 How does the life of a massive star end?

9 What is nuclear fusion?

Summary

Step 1 **Read the passage again and complete the outline with the words below.**

cycles / dust / dense / Milky Way / black / hydrogen / unique
birth / fusion / red giant / mass / white / supernova / gravity

I. Our galaxy, the ____________

A. Home to billions of stars, each ____________

B. Stars have life ____________ like humans

II. ____________ pulls

A. Clouds of gas and ____________ together

B. A ____________ ball (protostar) is formed

III. ____________ of a star

A. Nuclear ____________ makes a protostar glow

B. Burns until ____________ runs out

IV. Childhood to middle age of a star

A. Lifespan depends on ____________ of star

B. Transforms into a ____________ at the end of life cycle

V. End of star's life

A. Medium-sized stars become ____________ dwarves, then ____________ dwarves

B. Massive stars die with an explosion called a ____________ and create black holes

Step 2 **Complete the summary with your own words based on the outline.**

Our galaxy, the ____________, is home to billions of stars, and each one is ________.

____

____

____

____ The life of a massive red giant ends with an explosion called a ____________, which, in turn, generates a black hole.

Unit 20: Inventing the "Talkie"

Getting Started

1. Who is the person in the picture? Can you guess how he feels?
2. Can you explain what lip synching is?
3. Have you ever seen a silent film? What did you think?

Building Background Knowledge

The Jazz Singer

The 1927 American musical film *The Jazz Singer* is a landmark cinematic work, one that paved the way for the future commercial success of "talkies," or movies featuring synchronized sound. Based on a short story by Samson Raphaelson (his 1921 "The Day of Atonement"), this Warner Bros. film was the very first feature-length Hollywood "talkie" to incorporate synchronized dialogue into the dramatic action. The story revolves around a central character named Jakie Rabinowitz, whose decision to sing in a beer hall angers his traditional and devout Jewish father. After running away from home, Jakie makes a name for himself as a professional jazz singer, though he is still troubled by the conflicting pressures of his career and his heritage. *The Jazz Singer* generated $3.5 million in profits at the box office, and its success helped revolutionize the movie industry while signaling the coming decline of silent films.

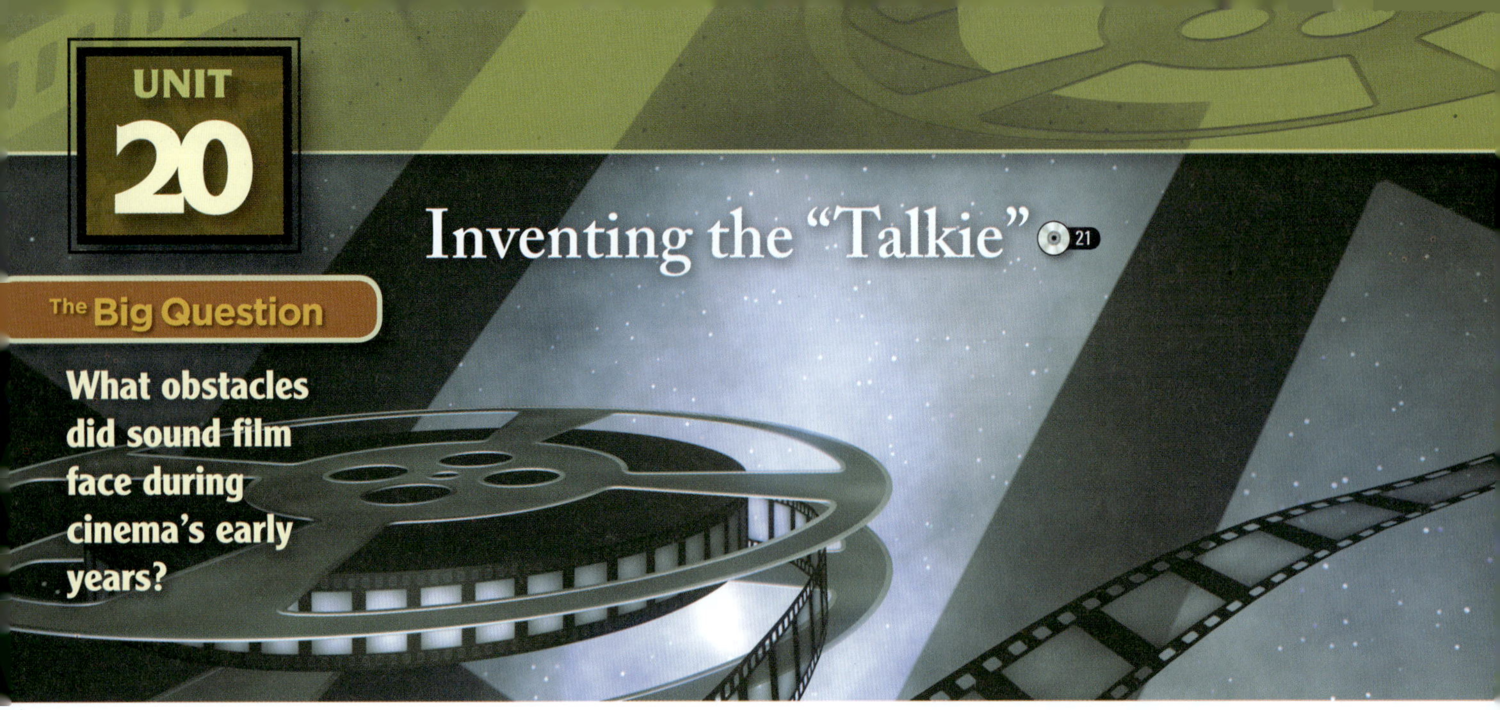

UNIT 20

Inventing the "Talkie"

The Big Question

What obstacles did sound film face during cinema's early years?

► Notes

During the earliest **era** of cinema, from the 1880s to the 1920s, films were silent. Any essential dialogue or background information was presented in the form of textual cards inserted between action scenes. Films were also enhanced by live music, from a full orchestra in the case of major **screenings** to a single pianist or guitarist in small-town theaters, and an announcer was sometimes employed to narrate the story when needed. Though the notion of silent film may seem limited from a modern perspective, filmmakers developed a unique **aesthetic**, and audiences were generally satisfied with the **medium**. Yet, throughout this period, inventors were continuously working on a means of combining picture with sound.

There were a few basic problems these inventors faced, the most troubling being synchronization: precisely aligning the audio with the video. Initial attempts to add sound utilized separate devices such as phonographs (early record players) to play tracks of music and sound effects to accompany the film. However, it was very difficult to ensure that the timing of the sound exactly matched what was being seen on the screen. **Amplification** was another limiting factor, for the technology to project recorded sound in large theaters with sufficient quality and volume simply did not exist.

The Kinetophone, designed by the Edison Manufacturing Company in 1895, was perhaps the first sound-film technology to be manufactured. It was based on the company's prior invention of the Kinetoscope, a cabinet-shaped device permitting single-person **viewing** of short films.

era a period of time with distinct characteristics
screening the presentation of a film
aesthetic a set of ideas concerning beauty
medium a means of communication
amplification the act of increasing the power of something

▸ Notes

In the Kinetophone, the motion-picture element was paired with a phonograph, so it suffered from synchronization issues. On the other hand, the fact that the Kinetophone had only to **accommodate** a single viewer meant amplification was not a **hindrance**. Unfortunately, this was also what led to the machine's abandonment, for by the turn of the century, filmmakers were coming to the realization that cinema was only **marketable** as a public offering.

▲ Kinetophone

It was not until the early 1920s that an innovation finally solved the problems associated with sound film. Called Phonofilm, it was invented by Lee De Forest and made use of a process by which sound could be recorded photographically onto a thin ribbon alongside the visual filmstrip. This ensured that, as long as sound and picture were correctly synchronized at the start of recording, they would remain in step throughout the film. De Forest's Phonofilm device also included mechanisms that amplified electrical signals, thus producing sounds full and loud enough to be projected to theater audiences.

Despite the advances made possible by Phonofilm, it took the 1927 release of *The Jazz Singer*, the first **feature-length** film to implement synchronized speech in addition to musical soundtracks, for the talking picture, or "talkie," to become a commercial success. All of the Hollywood studios responded to the triumph of *The Jazz Singer* by producing their own talkies and the popularity of the medium skyrocketed, pushing cinema into a new golden age.

On Your Own

How are today's films different from earlier movies like *The Jazz Singer*?

viewing the watching of a film
accommodate to be suitable for
hindrance something that makes it difficult to accomplish a goal
marketable capable of being easily sold
feature-length being the standard length of a movie

Vocabulary Building

[1-6] Complete each sentence with one of the words from the box.

ensure / device / continuously / despite / release / skyrocketed

1. He won the race ____________ the fact that his left shoelace was untied.

2. He invented a(n) ____________ that can detect the presence of radioactivity.

3. My favorite band's latest album ____________ was a great disappointment.

4. After working ____________ for three days, Jane finally took a break.

5. After the merger was announced, the value of the company's stock ____________.

6. You should leave 15 minutes early to ____________ that you're not late.

[7-12] Choose the words that are closest in meaning to the underlined ones.

7. We need to find a different <u>means</u> of staying in contact than the telephone.

a. amount b. reason c. area d. method

8. Steamed vegetables and a salad <u>accompany</u> the steak platter.

a. desert b. come with c. represent d. disagree with

9. We don't have <u>sufficient</u> funds to throw a holiday party this year.

a. rare b. enough c. limited d. sparse

10. Looking at it from a different <u>perspective</u>, I can see why David was angry with you.

a. age b. privacy c. view d. isolation

11. My <u>initial</u> reaction to the news was to scream, although I eventually calmed down.

a. ultimate b. latest c. first d. overwhelming

12. The spotlight <u>projected</u> a bright beam of light into the night sky.

a. gathered b. transmitted c. protected d. sketched

[13-15] Complete each sentence with the following idioms.

make use of / (be) associated with / on the other hand

13. I don't mind staying at home tonight; ________________, going out might be fun, too.

14. The new classroom ________________ all the latest educational technology.

15. Christmas season ________________ usually ________________ love and good will.

Reading Comprehension

1 What is the passage mainly about?

a. changes in the film market that brought about the introduction of "talkies"
b. the innovations that made possible the production of sound films
c. some of the drawbacks of the earliest silent films
d. technology that led to the success of the early cinema

2 How did audiences feel about silent films in the late 1800s and early 1900s?

a. They enjoyed the style that filmmakers had developed.
b. They preferred them to be accompanied by a full orchestra.
c. They were eager for them to be replaced by sound films.
d. They considered them to be amateur but entertaining.

3 Which aspect of the Kinetophone prevented its large-scale success?

a. its poor picture quality
b. its rejection of phonographs
c. its similarities to the Kinetoscope
d. its limited viewing capacity

4 The phrase in step in the passage is closest in meaning to

a. stuck b. pleasant
c. clear d. together

5 Which of the following was NOT used to introduce sound to film before the days of Phonofilm?

a. announcers that narrated the story
b. phonographs that played accompanying music and effects
c. in-theater orchestras and musicians
d. choirs of singers that performed dialogue

6 What can be inferred about 1920s sound films prior to *The Jazz Singer*?

a. Only a few of them were full-length films.
b. They did not include dialogue spoken by the actors.
c. Most of them did not utilize Phonofilm technology.
d. The majority were produced by Lee De Forest.

7 How did *The Jazz Singer* alter the course of cinematic history?

8 What was the Kinetophone designed to do?

9 How did De Forest's Phonofilm work?

Summary

Step 1 **Read the passage again and complete the outline with the words below.**

inventors / Kinetophone / silent film / failed / recorded / *The Jazz Singer*
synchronization / context / obstacles / amplification / phonographs / success

I. The age of ____________

A. Text cards, musicians, and announcers provided ____________ to films

B. The public was satisfied but ____________ were determined to create sound films

II. ____________ to sound film

A. ____________: the matching of sound to film action

B. ____________: projecting sound loudly and clearly enough in theaters

III. The ____________: the first sound-film technology

A. Used ____________, so synchronization was a problem

B. ____________ due to only being able to accommodate one viewer

IV. ____________ with De Forest's Phonofilm

A. ____________ sound photographically on the film and amplified it

B. ____________ popularized sound film and changed cinema history

Step 2 **Complete the summary with your own words based on the outline.**

During the age of ____________, text cards, musicians, and announcers were used to provide ____________ to films. ________________________

____

____

____

____________________________________ Benefiting from this technology, ____________ popularized sound film and changed cinema history.

Supplementary Material

(Write & Speak)

Unit 1

Write and Speak

The Big Question

Socrates gave up his life because he believed in the truth of his actions. Would you have made the same decision in his place? Why or why not?

A. Imagine you were in Socrates' shoes. What would you have done? Check (✔) the reasons for your choice. Write any other reasons you may have in the blanks.

Same decision	Different decision
☐ noble	☐ don't want to die
☐ send a message	☐ not worth it
☐ principles	☐ can't teach anymore
________	________

B. Explain why you chose what you did in A.

Your decision : ______________________________

Reason	Explanation

C. Using your ideas from Questions A and B, write a paragraph answering The Big Question at the top of this page. Share your answer with the class.

I would ____

____

____

____

____

____.

Unit 2

Write and Speak

The Big Question

Do you think Europe's expansion around the world should be viewed as primarily positive or primarily negative? Use reasons and examples to explain your answer.

A. Write the following ideas about the expansion of Europe in the correct columns. If you have more ideas, add them to each column.

- people killed
- people connected
- wealth created
- European diseases spread
- technological advances
- cultures destroyed
- global trade
- slavery

Positive	Negative

B. What do you think about the expansion of Europe in the 15th century? Do you think it had primarily positive or negative effects? Explain your choices with specific examples.

I think it had primarily ______________ effects.

Reason	Explanation

C. Using your ideas from Questions A and B, write a paragraph answering The Big Question at the top of this page. Share your answer with the class.

In my opinion, the expansion of Europe had ____

____

____

____

____

____.

Unit 3

Write and Speak

The Big Question

What do you think life would be like if Pangaea existed today? Give examples.

A. Look at the pictures below. Check (✔) how a world where we all lived in Pangaea would be different from our current world. Add some more ideas in the blanks.

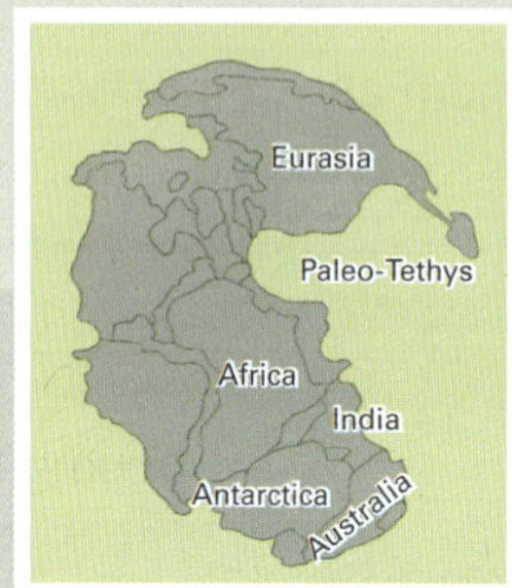

Differences

☐ fewer countries
☐ more trains
☐ less diversity of species
____

☐ no cargo ships
☐ more roads
☐ less diversity of food
____

B. Explain the reasons for your choices in A.

Idea	Explanation

C. Using your ideas from Questions A and B, write a paragraph answering The Big Question at the top of this page. Share your answer with the class.

If all the continents were attached, I think ______________________________
____
____
____
____
______________________________.

Unit 4

Write and Speak

The Big Question

Honey bees are affected by environmental problems just like all other creatures. Think of one environmental problem and describe how it could affect bees' ability to find food.

A. Check (✔) the problems or effects that you think affect honeybees. Write any other ideas you may have in the blank.

Environmental problems/effects

- ☐ air pollution
- ☐ global warming
- ☐ light pollution
- ☐ lack of sunlight
- ☐ habitat loss
- ☐ temperature changes
- ☐ new predators
- ____________________

B. Explain why the problems and effects you chose affect honeybees' ability to find food.

Environmental problem/effect	Reason

C. Using your ideas from Questions A and B, write a paragraph answering The Big Question at the top of this page. Share your answer with the class.

Global warming will probably affect honey bees in ____________________

____

____

____

____

____________________.

Unit 5

Write and Speak

The Big Question

Which invention do you think was more important, the modern printing press or the computer? Use reasons and specific examples to support your argument.

A. Check (✔) the points that you want to use in your argument. Write any other ideas you may have in the blanks.

Printing press

- ☐ popularized languages
- ☐ expanded knowledge
- ☐ improved literacy
- ☐ spread scientific ideas
- ☐ popularized books
- ________________

Computer

- ☐ improved communication
- ☐ increased access to information
- ☐ made life easier
- ☐ incorporated into many new technologies
- ☐ conserved paper
- ________________

B. Explain your choices in A.

I think the ____________ was a more important invention than the ____________.

Point	Explanation

C. Using your ideas from Questions A and B, write a paragraph answering The Big Question at the top of this page. Share your answer with the class.

I think ____

____

____

____

____

____.

Unit 6

Write and Speak

The Big Question

The discovery of the Rosetta Stone led to an explosion of interest and investment in the study of ancient Egypt. Why do people want to know about the past? Use specific reasons and examples to support your opinions.

A. Write the following reasons and ideas related to studying history in the correct columns. If you have more ideas, add them to each column.

- learn about one's culture
- better understand people and societies
- irrelevant
- waste of time and money
- learn from other's experiences

Important	NOT important

B. Explain your choices in A.

I think studying history is ______________________________.

Reason	Explanation with examples

C. Using your ideas from Questions A and B, write a paragraph answering The Big Question at the top of this page. Share your answer with the class.

I think studying history is ______________________________

____

____

____

____

____.

Unit 7

Write and Speak

The Big Question

If your country suddenly experienced a severe economic depression, how would you change your everyday behavior and habits in order to save money and survive? Use reasons and examples in your answer.

A. Check (✔) the ideas that you want to use in your answer. Write any other ideas you may have in the blank.

Changes

☐ less shopping
☐ plant a garden
☐ get two jobs
☐ fewer meals
☐ smaller house
☐ walk or bike

____

B. Explain the reasons for your choices in A.

Change	Explanation

C. Using your ideas from Questions A and B, write a paragraph answering The Big Question at the top of this page. Share your answer with the class.

In a severe economic depression, I would ______________________________

____

____

____

____

____.

Unit 8

Write and Speak

The Big Question

Imagine you live in an area hit by a hurricane or typhoon. Write a journal entry and share it with the class.

A. Write the following ideas about problems caused by storms and tasks that must be done to recover from them in the correct columns. If you have more ideas, add them to each column.

- flooding
- loss of electricity
- clean up houses and streets
- collapsing walls and bridges
- repair buildings
- bank up rivers
- blown over trees
- water shortages

Problems	Recovery

B. Choose and write the problems you would face and the tasks you'd have to perform from A.

Make up a name for the storm. ______________________________

Problem	What you would do to recover from the damage
•	
•	
•	

C. Using your ideas from Questions A and B, write your journal entry. Share your journal with the class.

____

____

____

____

____

____.

Unit 9

Write and Speak

The Big Question

Genetically modified foods are more helpful than harmful. Do you agree or disagree with this statement? Use reasons and examples in your answer.

A. Complete the cluster map about GM food with the ideas in the box. If you have more ideas, please write them down.

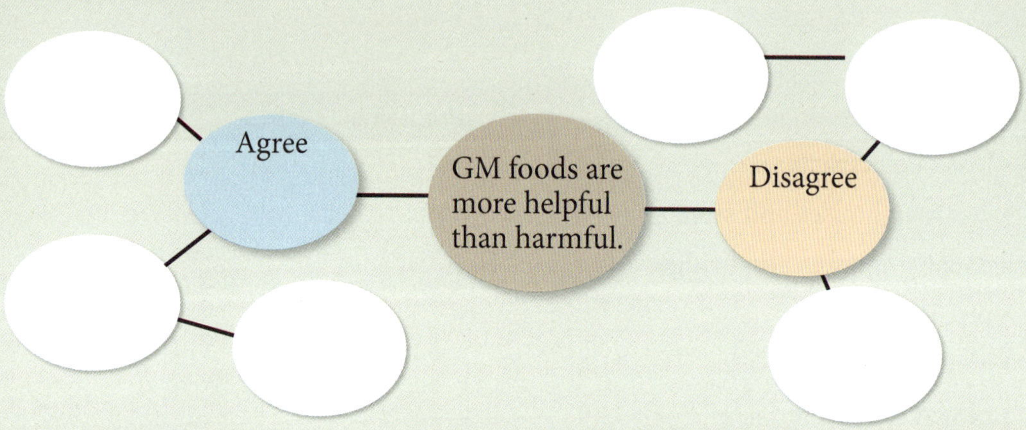

- increase crops
- too expensive
- could end hunger
- spread dangerous genes
- help farmers
- unknown health effects
- add nutrients
- cause allergies

B. Please write a paragraph answering The Big Question at the top of this page. Do you agree or disagree? Share your answer with the class.

Unit 10

Write and Speak

The Big Question

What spice or seasoning is the most influential in your country? Please introduce it to the class.

A. Check (✔) the spices that are commonly used in your country. If you have more ideas, please write them in the blank.

☐ red pepper
☐ sugar
☐ garlic
____

☐ black pepper
☐ ginger
☐ curry
☐ salt

B. Which is the most influential spice or seasoning among those above? Write about it in detail.

1. What is it? ______________
2. How does it taste? ______________
3. What kind of food is it used with? ______________
4. Why did you choose it as a crucial spice or seasoning in your country?
____

C. Using your ideas from Questions A and B, write a paragraph answering The Big Question at the top of this page. Share your answer with the class.

____
____
____
____
____
______________.

Unit 11

Write and Speak

The Big Question

Imagine that you were a Greek citizen during the time of Alexander the Great. Would you have chosen to settle in a faraway region of his empire? Why or why not?

A. Check (✔) the reasons that you want to use in your answer. Write any other ideas you may have in the blanks.

Yes	No
☐ curiosity	☐ dangerous
☐ jobs	☐ family
☐ travel	☐ security
☐ patriotism	☐ language/culture
____________	____________

B. Explain the reasons for your choices in A.

Reason	Explanation

C. Using your ideas from Questions A and B, write a paragraph answering The Big Question at the top of this page. Share your answer with the class.

If I were a Greek citizen living during the time of Alexander the Great, I would ________

____

____

____

____

____.

Unit 12

Write and Speak

The Big Question

Art influences people around the world. How are different forms of art important to society? Explain your answer in detail.

A. Check (✔) the forms of art you like. Then write a reason for each selection.

	YES	NO	Reason
1. paintings			
2. sculptures			
3. movies			
4. music			
5. books			

B. Write three ways in which art can influence people.

1. ______________________________
2. ______________________________
3. ______________________________

C. Using your ideas from Questions A and B, write a paragraph answering The Big Question at the top of this page. Share your answer with the class.

____
____
____
____
____
______________________________.

Unit 13

Write and Speak

The Big Question

Humans should do everything they can to save the Great Barrier Reef from destruction. Do you agree or disagree with this statement? Use reasons and examples to support your answer.

A. Check (✔) the points that you want to use in your argument. Write any other ideas you may have in the blanks.

Agree
- ☐ saving animals
- ☐ biodiversity
- ☐ living organism
- ☐ protect nature
- ______________

Disagree
- ☐ too expensive
- ☐ limiting human development
- ☐ impossible to save
- ☐ not important
- ______________

B. Explain the reasons for your choices in A.

Point	Explanation

C. Using your ideas from Questions A and B, write a paragraph answering The Big Question at the top of this page. Share your answer with the class.

____

____

____

____

____

____.

Unit 14

Write and Speak

The Big Question

Imagine living in Antarctica. What would you need to survive?

A. Check (✔) the items you would need to survive in Antarctica. Write any other items you might need in the blank.

Survival items

- ☐ bow and arrow
- ☐ firewood
- ☐ lighter
- ☐ skis
- ☐ tent
- ☐ compass
- ☐ shovel

____

B. Explain how the items you chose in A would help you survive in Antarctica.

Item	Survival use

C. Using your ideas from Questions A and B, write a paragraph answering The Big Question at the top of this page. Share your answer with the class.

If I were living in Antarctica, my primary needs would ______________________________

____

____

____

____

____.

Unit 15

Write and Speak

The Big Question

Would you want to live or work in a tall skyscraper? What would be the benefits or drawbacks?

A. Check (✔) the ideas that apply to your position. Write any other ideas you may have in the blanks.

Benefits

☐ Many neighbors
☐ Good views
☐ Luxurious
____

Drawbacks

☐ Expensive
☐ Inconvenient
☐ Dangerous
____

B. Explain the ideas for your choices in A.

Idea	Explanation

C. Using your ideas from Questions A and B, write a paragraph answering The Big Question at the top of this page. Share your answer with the class.

____
____
____
____
____
____.

Unit 16

Write and Speak

The Big Question

Many experts believe that placebos really work. Do you think that the mind can overcome all illnesses? Explain your answer in detail.

A. Please check (✔) the problems for which you think placebos would be effective. Then write a reason for each selection.

	YES	NO	Reason
1. common cold			
2. cancer			
3. heart attack			
4. allergies			
5. broken limbs			

B. Write three examples of how the mind can overcome matter.

1. ______________________________

2. ______________________________

3. ______________________________

C. Using your ideas from Questions A and B, write a paragraph answering The Big Question at the top of this page. Share your answer with the class.

Placebos have been scientifically proven to work. It is a case of mind over matter. The reason why the "placebo effect" takes place is ______________________________

____

____

____

______________________________.

Unit 17

Write and Speak

The Big Question

Green marketing is very important these days because many customers want to save the environment. Are you willing to spend more money to buy environmentally friendly products? Explain your answer in detail.

A. Please check (✔) the factors that you think are important when buying a product. Then briefly explain your reasons.

	YES	NO	Reason
1. color			
2. price			
3. company			
4. label			
5. environmentally friendly			

B. Using your ideas from Questions A, write a paragraph answering The Big Question at the top of this page. Share your answer with the class.

____

____

____

____

____

____.

Unit 18

Write and Speak

The Big Question

Some natural disasters can be predicted, but many cannot. What would be the benefits if all natural disasters could be accurately predicted? Explain your answer in detail.

A. Place a check (✔) next to the natural disasters you have experienced. Then briefly explain each experience.

		Explanation
1. earthquake	☐	
2. typhoon	☐	
3. drought	☐	
4. monsoon	☐	
5. blizzard	☐	

B. What are the first five things you would do in the case of a natural disaster?

1. ____________________
2. ____________________
3. ____________________
4. ____________________
5. ____________________

C. Using your ideas from Questions A and B, write a paragraph answering The Big Question at the top of this page. Share your answer with the class.

____

____

____

____

____

____________________.

Unit 19

Write and Speak

The Big Question

The life cycle of a star is very similar to that of a human being. In what ways are stars like people? Please explain in detail.

A. Please list some similarities and differences between a star's life and a human being's life. List the similarities in the middle and the differences in the outer areas.

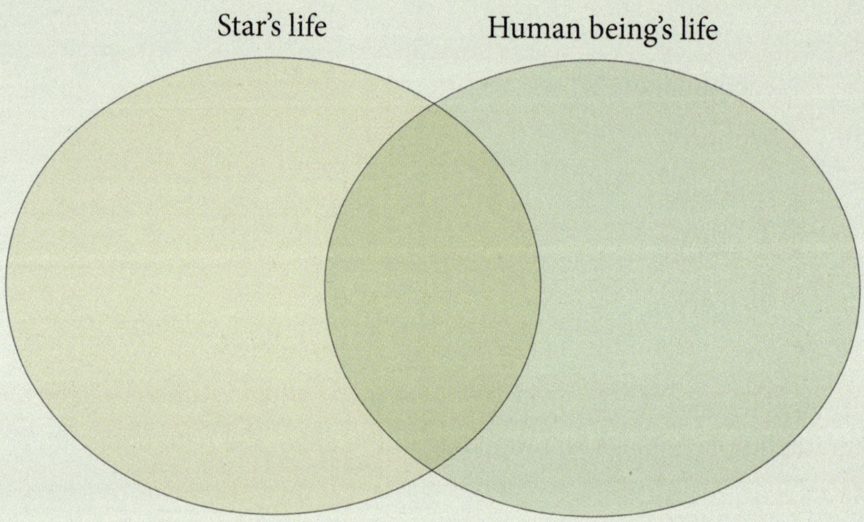

B. Using your ideas from Question A, write a paragraph answering The Big Question at the top of this page. Share your answer with the class.

Stars and humans have similar life cycles. ______________________________

Unit 20

Write and Speak

The Big Question

Would you have enjoyed watching movies without sound? Why or why not?

A. Check (✔) the ideas that you want to use in your argument. Write any other ideas you may have in the blanks.

Enjoy
- ☐ focus on visuals
- ☐ simpler stories
- ☐ live music
- ☐ more imagination
- ____________

Not enjoy
- ☐ hard to follow
- ☐ no sound effects
- ☐ difficult to read text cards
- ☐ boring
- ____________

B. Explain the reasons for your choices in A.

Idea	Explanation

C. Using your ideas from Questions A and B, write a paragraph answering The Big Question at the top of this page. Share your answer with the class.

I would ____

____

____

____

____

____.

Unit 1

Word	Definition	Translation
inconsistency	*n.* varying from one's stated principles *syn.* discrepancy	
recant	*v.* to take back a statement or opinion *syn.* withdraw	
manifestation	*n.* a sign of the existence of something *syn.* representation	
geometrical	*adj.* relating to the principles of geometry	
ascertain	*v.* to find out with an amount of certainty *syn.* identify	
sensory	*adj.* relating to the five senses	
dissect	*v.* to take apart and carefully analyze *syn.* examine	
essence	*n.* the true nature of something *syn.* spirit	
the cosmos	*n.* the universe, especially when it is thought of as an ordered system	
spirituality	*n.* the quality of being which is related to the spirit or soul *syn.* immateriality	
unyielding	*adj.* never stopping or giving in *syn.* constant	
argue	*v.* to put forth an idea *syn.* maintain	
drastically	*adv.* in a severe or intense manner *syn.* radically	
emphasis	*n.* the attachment of special interest or importance to something *syn.* stress	
indebted	*adj.* owing favor to someone for something received *syn.* grateful	
influential	*adj.* able to exert compelling force *syn.* important	
ravage	*v.* to thoroughly damage, especially by war *syn.* destroy	
talented	*adj.* showing great ability *syn.* gifted	
excel	*v.* to demonstrate above-average performance *syn.* succeed	
diminish	*v.* to become less in strength or amount *syn.* decrease	
assert	*v.* to state strongly and defend *syn.* argue	
encourage	*v.* to inspire and stimulate *syn.* support	
by no means	in no way; not at all	
put on trial	to examine someone's guilt or innocence through legal processes	
(be) found guilty	to be charged and sentenced for a crime in court	

Unit 2

Word	Definition	Translation
impetus	*n.* a force that stimulates a process or activity *syn.* motive	
feasible	*adj.* capable of being done *syn.* possible	
overland trade	*n.* commercial activity, especially between Europe and Asia	
endeavor	*n.* an attempt to do something in order to reach a goal *syn.* enterprise	
feature	*v.* to be a distinctive part of *syn.* star	
prominently	*adv.* in a major or important way *syn.* importantly	
expedition	*n.* a journey made for a specific purpose *syn.* trek	
exploration	*n.* the process of visiting an unknown territory for the purpose of discovery *syn.* investigation	
chart	*v.* to methodically traverse *syn.* explore	
extraction	*n.* the process of getting something, especially when some effort is involved *syn.* removal	
establish	*v.* to put in place or start up *syn.* organize	
migration	*n.* movement of people from one country or region to another *syn.* relocation	
transform	*v.* to modify the nature or form of something *syn.* change	
claim	*v.* to demand recognition of one's right to something *syn.* seize	
beneficial	*adj.* that which provides opportunity; favorable *syn.* advantageous	
impact	*n.* the force or influence of an event *syn.* effect	
acquire	*v.* to take into one's possession *syn.* obtain	
pursue	*v.* to try to achieve something *syn.* attempt	
signify	*v.* to be a sign of something *syn.* indicate	
found	*v.* to set up *syn.* establish	
consequence	*n.* the result of something that occurred earlier *syn.* repercussion	
eradicate	*v.* to completely abolish *syn.* destroy	
give rise to	to bring something about *syn.* cause	
carry out	to pull something off or make happen *syn.* execute	
along with	in addition to; with the help of	

Unit 3

Word	Definition	Translation
configuration	*n.* the relative positions of parts of a whole *syn.* arrangement	
stationary	*adj.* incapable of changing position *syn.* fixed	
hypothesize	*v.* to create a theory about something *syn.* theorize	
makeup	*n.* physical qualities that combine to form a being *syn.* composition	
frigid	*adj.* very cold in temperature *syn.* freezing	
theorize	*v.* to form a theory about *syn.* conjecture	
sonar	*n.* a technique used to locate objects underwater	
geology	*n.* the study of rocks and Earth's physical history	
mechanism	*n.* the method by which something occurs *syn.* means	
eon	*n.* an extremely long period of time *syn.* age	
ridge	*n.* a narrow, raised strip of hills or mountains	
spout	*v.* to flow forth in a stream or jet, often forcefully *syn.* spurt	
submerged	*adj.* below the surface of a liquid *syn.* underwater	
confirm	*v.* to establish the truth of something *syn.* certify	
massive	*adj.* great in size *syn.* enormous	
prehistoric	*adj.* that which existed before recorded history *syn.* ancient	
outlandish	*adj.* difficult to believe *syn.* outrageous	
possess	*v.* to have as a property or quality *syn.* contain	
dismiss	*v.* to disregard or brush aside *syn.* reject	
harden	*v.* to become hard, solid, or stiff *syn.* solidify	
demonstrate	*v.* to explain or manifest *syn.* show	
formalize	*v.* to make formal or clearly define *syn.* finalize	
break apart	to splinter; to divide into pieces	
account for	to explain the reason behind	
due to	because of	

Unit 4

Word	Definition	Translation
forager	*n.* one who wanders in search of food	
pollen	*n.* powdery yellow substance on flowers containing male reproductive cells	
artificial	*adj.* man-made; not found in nature *syn.* fake	
discern	*v.* to recognize or understand *syn.* perceive	
convey	*v.* to pass from one place to another *syn.* transmit	
source	*n.* a place from which something arises *syn.* origin	
sustenance	*n.* food that people or animals need in order to live	
waggle	*v.* to rock from side to side or back and forth *syn.* wobble	
loop	*v.* to move on a circular path *syn.* curve	
olfactory	*adj.* relating to the sense of smell	
intricate	*adj.* sophisticated; hard to understand *syn.* complex	
vicinity	*n.* the surrounding area *syn.* neighborhood	
acknowledge	*v.* to admit the truth of something *syn.* recognize	
dispute	*v.* to question the validity of *syn.* challenge	
concerning	*prep.* relating to something *syn.* regarding	
recruit	*v.* to seek one's services *syn.* engage	
utilize	*v.* to employ for a certain purpose *syn.* use	
located	*adj.* to be in a certain place *syn.* situated	
peculiar	*adj.* unusual and recognizable *syn.* distinctive	
assume	*v.* to take for granted without questioning *syn.* presume	
execute	*v.* to carry out *syn.* perform	
transmit	*v.* to pass something along *syn.* relay	
in addition to	besides; as well as	
draw the attention of	to attract	
in relation to	with respect to; relative to	

Unit 5

Word	Definition	Translation
commodity	*n.* a product or substance that is sold or bought *syn.* asset	
scribe	*n.* one who makes copies of books for a profession *syn.* copyist	
Dark Ages	*n.* the period of European history spanning 476 A.D. through 1000 A.D.	
literacy rate	*n.* the percentage of the population that can read and write	
carving	*n.* a design engraved into a surface *syn.* engraving	
metalsmith	*n.* one who works with metal	
alloy	*n.* a metal made by mixing two or more metals *syn.* compound	
pioneer	*v.* to prepare the way for and help introduce *syn.* inaugurate	
religious	*adj.* relating to religion in general or to a particular religion	
vernacular	*n.* the language or dialect of a certain region *syn.* native language	
contemporary	*adj.* occurring during the same time period *syn.* concurrent	
tediously	*adv.* in a manner that is tiresome or wearing *syn.* laboriously	
substantial	*adj.* large in quantity or scale *syn.* considerable	
delicate	*adj.* easily broken or damaged *syn.* fragile	
cover	*v.* to deal with as subject matter *syn.* contain	
evident	*adj.* easy to see; obvious *syn.* clear	
extensive	*adj.* comprehensive and thorough *syn.* lengthy	
notable	*adj.* worthy of discussion or notice *syn.* important	
eliminate	*v.* to do away with or get rid of *syn.* remove	
diffuse	*v.* to spread out away from the source *syn.* radiate	
fashion	*v.* to produce; to give form to *syn.* make	
employ	*v.* to make use of something *syn.* utilize	
in place of	instead of; as a replacement for	
usher in	to inaugurate; to start off	
deal with	to treat as subject matter	

Unit 6

Word	Definition	Translation
etch	*v.* to cut a design into a surface *syn.* scratch	
sacred	*adj.* endowed with spiritual or religious importance *syn.* divine	
artifact	*n.* an historically valuable item from the past *syn.* object	
inscription	*n.* text carved into a hard surface *syn.* carving	
commoner	*n.* a person who has no title of nobility *syn.* peasant	
decree	*n.* an order from an authority *syn.* declaration	
syntax	*n.* the appropriate order of words in sentences and phrases	
decipher	*v.* to figure out the meaning of something *syn.* deduce	
phonetic	*adj.* relating to the sounds produced when speaking	
archaeological	*adj.* relating to the study of historic cultures through their remains	
breakthrough	*n.* a sudden advance in knowledge *syn.* progress	
plentiful	*adj.* in great or sufficient supply *syn.* abundant	
specific	*adj.* definite or particular *syn.* certain	
fade	*v.* to gradually cease to exist *syn.* disappear	
represent	*v.* to express a concept through the use of a symbol *syn.* symbolize	
benefit	*v.* to derive advantage from *syn.* profit	
vanish	*v.* to fade away or come to an end, especially mysteriously *syn.* disappear	
cease	*v.* to discontinue or come to an end *syn.* stop	
uncover	*v.* to reveal or make clear *syn.* discover	
crack	*v.* to decipher or interpret *syn.* decode	
proficiency	*n.* the condition of being skilled in a certain field *syn.* ability	
achievement	*n.* something accomplished by special effort *syn.* accomplishment	
stand for	to represent	
be safe to say	to be very probable	
claim credit for	to announce that one is responsible for an achievement	

Unit 7

Word	Definition	Translation
recession	*n.* a period of economic slowdown *syn.* depression	
severity	*n.* harshness or hardness *syn.* intensity	
share	*n.* a fraction of the ownership of a company *syn.* stock	
cripple	*v.* to weaken or damage seriously *syn.* incapacitate	
savings	*n.* a quantity of money saved, especially in a bank account *syn.* funds	
withdrawal	*n.* the act of taking out money from a bank account	
funds	*n.* a supply of currency available for use *syn.* money	
mortgage	*n.* a loan used to purchase property	
institute	*v.* to put in place or set up *syn.* initiate	
federal	*adj.* relating to the central government of a nation *syn.* governmental	
afford	*v.* to have the financial means to do something *syn.* manage	
collapse	*n.* complete breakdown *syn.* failure	
compensate	*v.* to give money for something *syn.* pay	
evaporate	*v.* to dry up; vanish *syn.* disappear	
widespread	*adj.* far-reaching and widely distributed *syn.* prevalent	
intervention	*n.* the act of getting involved in an affair, especially to impede *syn.* interference	
prevail	*v.* to exist everywhere *syn.* abound	
plummet	*v.* to drop quickly *syn.* dive	
distribute	*v.* to give out *syn.* issue	
stem	*v.* to check the progress of something *syn.* stop	
generate	*v.* to bring into being *syn.* create	
halt	*v.* to bring to a stop *syn.* arrest	
needless to say	of course; obviously	
prior to	coming earlier in time	
place a ban on	to prohibit something	

Unit 8

Word	Definition	Translation
torrential	*adj.* occurring in large amounts and with great force *syn.* abundant	
extinct	*adj.* no longer in existence *syn.* dead	
meteorologist	*n.* a scientist who studies the weather	
phenomenon	*n.* an event in nature or society, especially something unusual *syn.* wonder	
terminology	*n.* the set of words used in a particular discipline *syn.* jargon	
sustained	*adj.* occurring without slowing or stopping *syn.* unflagging	
shaft	*n.* a long, narrow vertical passage	
girth	*n.* the measurement of the distance around something	
spiral	*n.* a shape made up of interconnected loops *syn.* coil	
spawn	*v.* to make something happen or develop *syn.* create	
devastating	*adj.* causing great harm *syn.* destructive	
tremendous	*adj.* a great amount *syn.* huge	
flood	*v.* to cover in water	
minimize	*v.* to keep to the smallest amount possible	
orbit	*v.* to move around something in a circular motion *syn.* circle	
unleash	*v.* to let loose something powerful *syn.* release	
dense	*adj.* possessing a high level of density *syn.* thick	
violent	*adj.* characterized by unrestrained force *syn.* destructive	
bestow	*v.* to officially give something, such as a title *syn.* award	
extend	*v.* to reach out across a distance *syn.* reach	
ample	*adj.* existing in a large enough amount *syn.* sufficient	
dispense	*v.* to give out	
result in	to lead to something *syn.* cause	
regardless of	occurring or existing in spite of something *syn.* despite	
not surprisingly	as expected	

Unit 9

Word	Definition	Translation
selective breeding	*n.* the process of breeding to achieve desirable traits	
resilient	*adj.* able to deal with adversity *syn.* adaptable	
strain	*n.* a genetically related group with specific traits	
profile	*n.* a description of a thing or person	
characteristic	*n.* a quality that distinguishes someone or something *syn.* trait	
cold spell	*n.* a period of lower than normal temperatures	
drought	*n.* a period with an extreme shortage of rainfall	
produce	*n.* food grown in large quantities to be sold	
pharmaceutical	*adj.* related to the production of medicines	
controversy	*n.* a dispute with intense reactions on both sides	
advantage	*n.* a quality that makes success more likely *syn.* edge	
shortcut	*n.* a way of doing something in less time than usual	
regulate	*v.* to make something conform to rules or laws *syn.* manage	
ultimately	*adv.* in the end *syn.* finally	
contamination	*n.* the introduction of unwanted elements *syn.* pollution	
adverse	*adj.* unpleasant or causing harm *syn.* unfavorable	
alter	*v.* to cause a change in something *syn.* change	
desirable	*adj.* having qualities that are sought after *syn.* advantageous	
insert	*v.* to put into something *syn.* put	
transfer	*v.* to move something to a different location *syn.* relocate	
implant	*v.* to fix something deep within something else *syn.* embed	
embrace	*v.* to react favorably to something *syn.* welcome	
for the time being	being the case currently, but only temporarily	
in place of	as a substitute for something else	
bring about	to cause to happen	

Unit 10

Word	Definition	Translation
agent	*n.* something used to achieve a particular purpose *syn.* medium	
preservation	*n.* the process of keeping something from decaying	
millennia	*n.* thousands of years	
evaporate	*v.* to change into vapor *syn.* dissolve	
proximity	*n.* the state of being near something *syn.* nearness	
motivator	*n.* something that makes you want to do something *syn.* instigator	
riverine	*adj.* relating to a river	
affluence	*n.* a large amount of money or valuable goods *syn.* wealth	
monopoly	*n.* exclusive control of an industry or market by only one person or group	
fuel	*v.* to increase in intensity *syn.* sustain	
throughout	*adv.* from start to finish	
remove	*v.* to take something out of something else *syn.* extract	
note	*v.* to perceive something *syn.* observe	
secure	*v.* to get something through great effort *syn.* obtain	
wage	*v.* to carry out a war or battle *syn.* conduct	
prominence	*n.* the state of being widely known and having great influence *syn.* importance	
pivotal	*adj.* strongly influencing the course of events *syn.* crucial	
abundant	*adj.* existing in great numbers *syn.* plentiful	
thrive	*v.* to exist in a strong and healthy state *syn.* flourish	
dominate	*v.* to have power over *syn.* control	
principal	*adj.* most important *syn.* main	
prolific	*adj.* creating something in large amounts *syn.* productive	
pick up	to raise into the air *syn.* lift	
set out to	to begin something with a specific goal in mind	
take for granted	to use something without thought or gratitude	

Unit 11

Word	Definition	Translation
epoch	*n.* a specific period in history *syn.* era	
dominance	*n.* the condition of being powerful *syn.* rule	
prowess	*n.* exceptional ability or skill	
subsequently	*adv.* happening after *syn.* later	
host	*v.* to provide a place for *syn.* accommodate	
ponder	*v.* to think deeply about something *syn.* contemplate	
ethical	*adj.* conforming to the standards of what is deemed right *syn.* moral	
advance	*n.* progress in development *syn.* improvement	
discipline	*n.* an area of knowledge that people study *syn.* subject	
vestige	*n.* a remainder of something that once existed *syn.* trace	
advocate	*v.* to argue in support of something *syn.* bolster	
abandon	*v.* to reject or give up *syn.* discard	
emerge	*v.* to appear for the first time *syn.* evolve	
accessible	*adj.* easy to understand or appreciate *syn.* attainable	
elaborate	*v.* to build upon or add details to *syn.* embellish	
whereas	*conj.* while in contrast *syn.* while	
depict	*v.* to create an image of something *syn.* represent	
significant	*adj.* great in scale or impact *syn.* major	
profit	*v.* to gain an advantage or earn money *syn.* benefit	
maintain	*v.* to continue the existence of something *syn.* preserve	
adopt	*v.* to practice and use *syn.* embrace	
formulate	*v.* to develop methodically *syn.* devise	
call for	to request or demand	
divorce from	to put distance between or separate from	
hold sway	to dominate or influence	

Unit 12

Word	Definition	Translation
movement	*n.* a group of people who work together to obtain a certain objective *syn.* trend	
impression	*n.* an image in the mind inspired by some stimulus *syn.* perception	
brushstroke	*n.* the mark left by a brush	
fleeting	*adj.* disappearing quickly *syn.* temporary	
optical	*adj.* related to vision and the eyes *syn.* visual	
pigment	*n.* a substance that contributes color *syn.* colorant	
exhibition	*n.* a display of art *syn.* show	
Pointillism	*n.* a style of painting that produces images with many small dots of color	
Cubism	*n.* 20th century style of painting that was geometrical and abstract	
Expressionism	*n.* colorful and symbolic style of painting representing the artist's inner experience	
apply	*v.* to make use of *syn.* use	
impulsively	*adj.* affected by a feeling or emotional state *syn.* spontaneously	
expressive	*adj.* showing emotion or conveying an idea *syn.* meaningful	
critic	*n.* someone who writes about and evaluates artistic works *syn.* analyst	
scene	*n.* what is shown in a picture *syn.* picture	
bustling	*adj.* full of energy *syn.* lively	
profound	*adj.* of deep significance *syn.* deep	
portray	*v.* to depict by painting *syn.* represent	
unsophisticated	*adj.* not refined *syn.* simple	
formal	*adj.* related to the organization or composition of the elements in a work of art *syn.* structured	
flourish	*v.* to be successful and prosper *syn.* thrive	
appreciate	*v.* to hold in high esteem *syn.* value	
owing to	as a result of	
mean to	to intend	
in advance	ahead of time	

Unit 13

Word	Definition	Translation
cylindrical	*adj.* shaped like a cylinder	
ingest	*v.* to take something into one's body *syn.* consume	
algae	*n.* a simple form of plant life that lives in water	
photosynthesis	*n.* a process used by plants to create its own food	
harbor	*v.* to provide a place or habitat for something *syn.* safeguard	
excrete	*v.* to naturally remove something from one's body *syn.* discharge	
microorganism	*n.* a tiny living creature	
mollusk	*n.* a type of sea or land animal that has a soft body usually covered by a hard shell	
designation	*n.* the official categorization of something *syn.* classification	
runoff	*n.* excess liquid exceeding storage capacity *syn.* overflow	
transparent	*adj.* easily seen through *syn.* see-through	
attract	*v.* to entice something to approach *syn.* draw	
presence	*n.* physical proximity	
strict	*adj.* not flexible *syn.* rigid	
contaminate	*v.* to cause something to become impure *syn.* poison	
permit	*v.* to allow something to occur *syn.* allow	
mutually	*adv.* experienced by two people or things	
mitigate	*v.* to lessen the severity of something *syn.* diminish	
extraordinary	*adj.* beyond standard expectations *syn.* remarkable	
serve	*v.* to behave in the manner of something else *syn.* act	
curb	*v.* to restrain something *syn.* restrict	
prolonged	*adj.* occurring over a long period of time *syn.* extended	
in turn	as the next step in a process	
die off	to cease living en masse	
lead to	to make something happen *syn.* cause	

Unit 14

Word	Definition	Translation
arid	*adj.* characterized by scarcity of water *syn.* dry	
region	*n.* a large area of land *syn.* area	
inhospitable	*adj.* not accommodating for life *syn.* unfriendly	
habitat	*n.* the area where a plant or animal lives *syn.* environment	
inhabitant	*n.* someone or something that lives in an area *syn.* resident	
field	*n.* an area of study or investigation *syn.* subject	
treaty	*n.* an official document of understanding *syn.* agreement	
infringe	*v.* to violate something that is not one's own *syn.* intrude	
radioactive	*adj.* having the ability to produce harmful energy *syn.* toxic	
presage	*v.* to warn of a future event *syn.* foreshadow	
diverse	*adj.* of different sorts or varieties *syn.* various	
permanent	*adj.* lasting indefinitely *syn.* continuous	
hover	*v.* to linger near *syn.* remain	
blanket	*v.* to cover with a layer, like a blanket *syn.* cover	
preserve	*v.* to protect from destruction *syn.* safeguard	
absolutely	*adv.* with no exception *syn.* entirely	
frigid	*adj.* characterized by extremely low temperatures *syn.* cold	
plunge	*v.* to drop rapidly *syn.* fall	
harness	*v.* to make use of *syn.* utilize	
consume	*v.* to ingest *syn.* eat	
engage	*v.* to actively take part in something	
severe	*adj.* great in scale or intensity *syn.* major	
a number of	an unspecified large amount	
make up	to account for *syn.* define	
for the sake of	in order to benefit someone or something	

Unit 15

Word	Definition	Translation
skyscraper	*v.* a tall commercial building	
vertical	*adj.* positioned at an angle of 90° to the horizon *syn.* upright	
masonry	*n.* stone or brick structures	
necessitate	*v.* to make necessary or essential *syn.* require	
impede	*v.* to be an obstacle *syn.* obstruct	
skeleton	*n.* internal structure that provides support *syn.* framework	
manner	*n.* way of doing something *syn.* method	
towering	*adj.* reaching a great height *syn.* tall	
compartment	*n.* a small enclosed space *syn.* box	
address	*v.* to turn one's attention to or deal with something *syn.* undertake	
flexibility	*n.* the capacity to bend without breaking *syn.* pliability	
once	*conj.* as soon as *syn.* when	
available	*adj.* ready for immediate use *syn.* accessible	
bulky	*adj.* comparatively large in size *syn.* big	
impose	*v.* to put on or thrust upon *syn.* demand	
define	*v.* to function as a prominent characteristic *syn.* distinguish	
bear	*v.* to hold up or endure *syn.* support	
scarce	*adj.* that which is uncommon or difficult to find *syn.* rare	
function	*v.* to perform a certain role *syn.* act	
lower	*v.* to move something in a downward direction	
descend	*v.* to go down *syn.* fall	
swell	*v.* to expand or increase in amount *syn.* grow	
in place	properly arranged; in the correct position	
keep out	to prevent from entering	
out of control	impossible to stop or restrain	

Unit 16

Word	Definition	Translation
inert	*adj.* having no drug-like effect *syn.* inactive	
saline solution	*n.* salt water	
skepticism	*n.* the state of not believing *syn.* doubt	
generic	*adj.* not having a brand name or manufacturer *syn.* unspecific	
disorder	*n.* a physical or mental problem *syn.* illness	
side effect	*n.* a negative accompanying effect of a drug	
nausea	*n.* the state of being sick to the stomach and feeling the need to vomit	
drowsiness	*n.* the state of being sleepy *syn.* tiredness	
rash	*n.* irritation of the skin	
prescribe	*v.* to specify a treatment for a patient	
approval	*n.* formal permission *syn.* acceptance	
phenomenon	*n.* something that is exceptional *syn.* wonder	
undesirable	*adj.* not wanted *syn.* negative	
coincidence	*n.* occurrence by chance *syn.* chance	
uncanny	*adj.* beyond the normal *syn.* extraordinary	
stimulating	*adj.* exciting the body or senses *syn.* invigorating	
fascinate	*v.* to attract the interest and curiosity of *syn.* absorb	
treat	*v.* to help cure a disease *syn.* heal	
merely	*adv.* nothing more than *syn.* just	
convince	*v.* to make someone believe something *syn.* persuade	
hinder	*v.* to stop from happening *syn.* prevent	
outcome	*n.* final result *syn.* consequence	
motivate	*v.* to provide with a reason to do something *syn.* prompt	
trigger	*v.* to cause to begin *syn.* initiate	
genuine	*adj.* not fake *syn.* real	

Unit 17

Word	Definition	Translation
advent	*n.* the beginning of something *syn.* onset	
trend	*n.* something popular at a given time *syn.* fad	
ecologically	*adv.* in a manner related to nature *syn.* environmentally	
environmentally friendly	*adj.* not causing harm to nature *syn.* green	
sloppy	*adj.* unorganized and of poor quality *syn.* careless	
packaging	*n.* the material in which something is wrapped	
hemp	*n.* a type of plant that is used to make rope and strong rough cloth	
motivator	*n.* something that makes you want to achieve something	
certification	*n.* official validation	
purchase	*n.* the act of buying something	
conservation	*n.* the preservation of something	
implement	*v.* to put into action	
falsely	*adv.* in a deceptive manner *syn.* dishonestly	
ignorance	*n.* a lack of knowledge or information	
chain	*n.* many similar businesses with one owner	
practice	*n.* a form or manner of doing something	
discern	*v.* to notice and properly identify *syn.* detect	
excessive	*adj.* more than is needed or wanted	
intentional	*adj.* done on purpose *syn.* calculated	
wary	*adj.* distrustful and careful *syn.* cautious	
ultimately	*adv.* in the end *syn.* finally	
indeed	*adv.* in truth or reality *syn.* actually	
jump on the bandwagon	to follow a trend or fad	
look out for	to be careful to avoid	
take on	to dedicate oneself to achieving a goal	

Unit 18

Word	Definition	Translation
erupt	*v.* to eject molten rock, ash, and gas from a volcano *syn.* explode	
seismic	*adj.* relating to the vibration of the Earth	
deformation	*n.* changes in Earth's crust resulting from geologic processes	
crust	*n.* the rocky outer layer of the Earth	
molten rock	*n.* rock under the Earth's surface that has been heated to its melting point	
rupture	*n.* a state of being broken *syn.* rift	
sulphur dioxide	*n.* a toxic gas emitted by a volcano	
crater	*n.* a hole at the opening of a volcano *syn.* depression	
infrared telescope	*n.* a telescope that detects heat	
tiltmeter	*n.* a tool that measures small changes in the slope of Earth's crust	
indicator	*n.* evidence of something *syn.* sign	
remote	*adj.* located at a distance *syn.* offsite	
estimate	*v.* to make an approximate judgment *syn.* calculate	
transmit	*v.* to communicate through radio signals *syn.* send	
crawl	*v.* to move slowly and carefully *syn.* creep	
release	*v.* to put out *syn.* emit	
approximately	*adv.* just about *syn.* around	
minute	*adj.* extremely small *syn.* tiny	
magnitude	*n.* greatness of scale *syn.* extent	
detect	*v.* to discover the presence of *syn.* sense	
abnormal	*adj.* deviating from the ordinary *syn.* unusual	
emit	*v.* to give off *syn.* issue	
thanks to	because of; due to	
keep an eye out for	to monitor; to scan for	
figure out	to determine; to calculate	

Unit 19

Word	Definition	Translation
galaxy	*n.* a cluster of stars held together by gravity	
creature	*n.* a living being (usually other than a human) *syn.* organism	
dust	*n.* a cloud of small, fine particles *syn.* granules	
asteroid	*n.* a small planet that orbits the sun especially between Mars and Jupiter	
particle	*n.* a small component of matter	
fusion	*n.* in physics, a reaction in which atoms join	
mass	*n.* in physics, the property of matter which results in it having weight *syn.* size	
dwarf	*n.* in astronomy, a small star of average brightness	
stellar	*adj.* relating to stars	
void	*n.* an empty area of space where nothing exists	
element	*n.* a substance that cannot be chemically separated into component substances	
contract	*v.* to pull inward or shrink *syn.* condense	
leftover	*adj.* an unused quantity *syn.* remaining	
dense	*adj.* being highly concentrated *syn.* compact	
expand	*v.* to grow larger in size *syn.* enlarge	
reaction	*n.* the joining of atoms *syn.* fusion	
reach	*v.* to arrive at a certain point *syn.* attain	
eventually	*adv.* after a period of time *syn.* finally	
core	*n.* the innermost part of a celestial body *syn.* center	
smash	*v.* to collide forcefully *syn.* crash	
stick	*v.* to remain attached *syn.* adhere	
incredible	*adj.* so extraordinary that it is difficult to believe *syn.* unbelievable	
run out of	to use up or finish a supply of something *syn.* exhaust	
fall apart	to break into pieces *syn.* collapse	
go through	to progress through *syn.* undergo	

Unit 20

Word	Definition	Translation
era	*n.* a period of time with distinct characteristics *syn.* age	
screening	*n.* the presentation of a film *syn.* showing	
aesthetic	*n.* a set of ideas concerning beauty	
medium	*n.* a means of communication	
amplification	*n.* the act of increasing the power of something	
viewing	*n.* the watching of a film	
accommodate	*v.* to be suitable for *syn.* fit	
hindrance	*n.* something that makes it difficult to accomplish a goal *syn.* obstacle	
marketable	*adj.* capable of being easily sold	
feature-length	*adj.* being the standard length of a movie	
ensure	*v.* to make sure something happens *syn.* guarantee	
device	*n.* a tool with a specific purpose *syn.* gadget	
continuously	*adv.* without stopping *syn.* constantly	
despite	*prep.* in spite of *syn.* although	
release	*n.* the act of making something available to consumers	
skyrocket	*v.* to increase quickly and greatly *syn.* soar	
means	*n.* a way of accomplishing something *syn.* method	
accompany	*v.* to go along with	
sufficient	*adj.* high enough in quantity or quality to meet a need *syn.* enough	
perspective	*n.* a particular way of looking at something *syn.* view	
initial	*adj.* occurring at the start *syn.* beginning	
project	*v.* to send outward *syn.* transmit	
make use of	to use something for a particular purpose	
(be) associated with	to be related to	
on the other hand	looked at from another point of view	

LEVEL GUIDE NE_Build & Grow Products

Category	Level	Kindergarten	Low Beginner	Beginner	High Beginner	Low Intermediate	Intermediate	High Intermediate	Secondary A	Secondary B	Secondary C	Word Count
	Lexile®	BR~120L	120L~350L		350L~600L		500L~850L		750L~950L		700L~1100L	
	CEFR Level	Pre~A1	A1		A2			B1		B2		
	AR Reading Level (Average)	0.5	1.3	2.0	2.5	3.3	3.7	4.5	5.2	5.8	6.7	
Phonics	Phonics Code											
	Phonics Show											
	Come On, Phonics											
Readers	Show Time Level 1											400~600
	Show Time Level 2											550~1100
	Show Time Level 3											800~1200
Course-book	Come On, Everyone											
Reading	Read It! 30											30~45
	Read It! 40											35~50
	Read It! 50											50~65
	Read It! 60											50~65
	Read It! 80											65~95
	Read It! 100											70~100
	Read It! 150											100~150
	Read It! 200											160~220
	Read It! 250											220~300
	Reading Sketch Starter											30~45
	Reading Sketch											35~65
	Reading Sketch Up											80~100
	Reading Sponge											45~70
	Read & Retell											50~80
	Reading Sense											80~100
	Reading Clue											100~130
	The Basic Way											150~240
	Read to Reach											140~220
	Reading Source											140~200
	The Best Way											230~340
	Reading Peak											190~270
	Read Up											350~500
	Easy Link Starter											20~35
	Easy Link											35~80
	Insight Link Starter											80~120
	Insight Link											120~250
	Subject Link Starter											90~135
	Subject Link											140~360
	Subject Link Starter 2nd Edition											90~135
	Subject Link 2nd Edition											140~290

Category	Level	Kindergarten	Low Beginner	Beginner	High Beginner	Low Intermediate	Intermediate	High Intermediate	Secondary A	Secondary B	Secondary C	Word Count
	Lexile®	BR~120L	120L~350L		350L~600L		500L~850L		750L~950L		700L~1100L	
	CEFR Level	Pre~A1	A1		A2			B1		B2		
	AR Reading Level (Average)	0.5	1.3	2.0	2.5	3.3	3.7	4.5	5.2	5.8	6.7	
Listening	Listening Stage Starter											
	Listening Stage											
	Listening Stage Plus											
	Listening Seed											
	Listening Season											
	Listening Planner											
Writing	Write It! Beginner											
	Write It!											
	Write It! Paragraph to Essay											
	Write Right Beginner											
	Write Right											
	Write Right Paragraph to Essay											
Speaking	Speaking Stage Starter											
	Speaking Stage											
	Speaking Stage Plus											
	Everyone, Speak! Kids											
	Everyone, Speak! Beginner											
	Everyone, Speak!											
Grammar	중학 영문법 Link											
	요즘 초등 영문법											
	Grammar Stage Starter											
	Grammar Stage											
	Grammar Stage Plus											
	Grammar Ten 기초											
	Grammar Ten 기본											
	Grammar Ten 완성											
	Grammar Space Kids											
	Grammar Space Beginner											
	Grammar Space											
	Grammar in Mind											
	Grammar in Focus											
	Grammar Effect											
Voca-bulary	Word Up											400~1200
	요즘 초등 영단어											216~222
Assess-ment	RADIX Reading / Listening for the TOEFL iBT Blue & Black											